ADAMS COUNTY BIGFOOT

FRIEND OR BEAST?

JAY VERNON

HANGAR 1 PUBLISHING

CONTENTS

INTRODUCTION

I want to tell you my life story, of what seemed to be a normal life for a boy growing up on a farm in central Wisconsin from 1968 until 1984. It wasn't until I was almost seventeen that I realized that my life had been far from normal. With so many unexplainable strange happenings, I now wonder, "*was I in danger the whole time*?" How did I not see what was really going on? These are the incidents that I clearly remember. I'm one hundred percent sure that I didn't notice every sign throughout my childhood. I was literally oblivious to what I was really seeing and hearing. I never thought for a second that it wasn't a human. Boy, was I wrong!

1

NEW BEGINNINGS

Age 2

I t was a sunny, steamy August day in 1968. I was almost three years old at the time. We were moving from Milwaukee three hours north to an unincorporated town of Briggsville, Wisconsin. It was the first time to our new, or should I say, a very old farm that my father was so interested in having after his retirement from the military. He had always wanted to go back to the way of life he had grown up with. He was raised on a small farm in central Alabama until he was fifteen. Their farm had a few farm animals, crops and even a small cotton field. After enlisting at the young age of sixteen, he then spent the next twenty-two years in the Army and Navy as a parachute rigger. That's a person who makes parachutes. My parents met while my dad was on leave touring Central Park in New York City. My mom was there for her senior class theater trip. My parents' story goes that a strange man that my mom had no interest in was hitting on her as they were enjoying Central Park. She was telling the man to please leave her alone. The strange man kept stopping her and her friends stating that she was the most beautiful woman he had ever seen. My dad, who was walking by with another Army friend, saw my mom's frustration with this man and stepped in pretending to be her boyfriend. The man then finally left her alone. My mom thanked my dad and they started talking.

Before you knew it, my mom and dad had hit it off right away. They kept in contact, dated and were married a year later in Alexandria, Virginia, where my father was stationed. After a few years of trying, they thought that they couldn't have children. They were saddened that they couldn't have the family they deeply wanted. After giving up on having children, they were approached by a military friend of my dad's that felt he and his wife couldn't care for their newborn. They knew my parent's situation and asked my parents to adopt their baby boy. My parents thought long and hard and decided to adopt him and make him their own. This baby became my brother Wayne. About two years later, they were surprised to find out they were pregnant with my brother Drew in 1961. With the two children in tow, my mother followed my father to every stateside assignment he had. After Alexandria, they moved to Alameda, California, San Diego and then to Pensacola, Florida, where I was born in 1965. Six months after I was born, my father decided to retire from the military and concede to my mother's wishes and move to the Milwaukee area where she had grown up. My mom really wanted to just settle down after moving around the country so much. They took all their savings and built a rather nice new home in Browndeer, a suburb just north of Milwaukee. A year later, my third brother Lonnie was born on Christmas Day in 1966. My mother loved the new home and being close to her family and the friends she grew up with.

In the summer of '68, my father couldn't take the city life and decided to pack the family up and move them to an old farm in the deep woods of central Wisconsin just outside of the unincorporated town of Briggsville. It was a quaint little fishing town with a nice lake, a gas station, a tiny Post Office, two Church's, one Lutheran and the other Catholic, a General Store where you could get almost anything. Besides the normal small selection of canned and dry foods, they had building materials, farm supplies and parts, feed for any farm animal, fishing supplies and so on. There were two taverns, The Mill Inn and the Pheasant Inn, just across the street from each other. There also was a VFW Hall just across the street from the Mill Inn. There was a four-room school for grades K through 6th grade and just on the north side of town was a sandy baseball diamond, a place that I would come to know well. Head three miles north out of town past that ball diamond, past a few other farms, and that's where we were moving to. It had belonged to a brother to another farmer about a mile down the road. He had died in an accident when a twelve-point buck had jumped over the road and its horns had penetrated his heart after crashing through the windshield, killing him instantly. After his death, the farm had gone up for sale and my father bought it without even asking my mother.

My father had taken a U-Haul up to the farm a few days ahead with my two older brothers, Wayne and Drew, to clean up the farm and start moving in. That summer day when my mother, my little brother Lonnie and I pulled into the sandy driveway was the beginning of our new lives.

My mother looked for the first time upon an old, white, rickety, two-story farmhouse that was built in the mid-1800s. The farmhouse had a kitchen built off the side that was added on around 1900. It was obvious why she was crying for several minutes with both hands on the steering wheel. This old run-down farmhouse was the opposite of the new house she had just left behind in the city.

My father came out from behind the house and eagerly waved her up the drive. She wiped her eyes and eventually pulled the rest of the way into the drive. As she got out, she grabbed Lonnie from the back seat and followed my dad around as he gave her the tour. I quickly jumped out and started to explore the property. In the front yard was a large oak tree that shaded the house. Across the driveway were a big red barn with a rock foundation wall painted white and a chicken coop behind the house, a granary, and a corn crib. Behind the barn was a tall brick feed silo with a metal top and a ladder fastened up the side all the way to the top. The buildings were all old and run down. There was a sandy dirt trail that ran around the back

3

of the house and between the buildings. Next to the barn were about ten dairy cows in one pen and six pigs in another. Then I couldn't believe what I saw...there were five horses in a back pen with a horse shelter to the side. I had seen horses before in a parade in Milwaukee, but these were our very own! They were an assortment of sizes and colors. Behind the barn were an old orange Allis Chalmers tractor and corn picker. What young boy doesn't love tractors and horses! I was very excited! My life on the farm is just starting! There was something new to check out around every corner. So much room to run around and be a kid. Who knows what tomorrow will bring!

2

FIRST DAY

Age 2

I woke up our first day on the farm to the smell of pancakes and bacon my mother was cooking! The sun was shining brightly through all the windows that had no curtains in the entire house. It was rare seeing my father at the table eating with us. He normally was at work when we lived in Browndeer. He had been a Security Officer at the local mall and did Private Investigating work. So, he wasn't around much the couple of years we lived there. I couldn't wait to finish eating so I could go out and explore the farm more. I especially wanted to see the horses!

My father had plans for Wayne and Drew to help fix up and clean out the buildings on the farm. I followed them outside, and my father hadn't noticed that I went off by the horses just across the driveway. I was a quiet yet somewhat fearless kid that loved to explore my surroundings. I reached through the fence and started petting the horses. Their noses were so soft! Drew yelled to me, stating, "They'll bite your fingers off!" I didn't pay much attention since both of my older brothers loved to pick on me. After a few minutes, I thought I would peak into the barn to find nothing inside the lower floor. It smelled like cow manure. I really didn't like bad smells, so I quickly moved on. I walked around to the back side of the barn and found a tractor ramp to the hayloft. I followed the ramp into the open loft door. The musty smell of the hay bales was strong. You could see the sunlight peaking between all the boards. There were huge beams across the upper area of the loft that reached from one end to the other. Hanging from the ceiling was a long rope with a small board tied to the end. It was a swing that would allow you to swing out the front hayloft door. I thought, *"Wow, this was a cool place to hang out."* Then I heard my name being yelled. I ran out of the barn to find my father with a great look of anger on his face. He yelled, "I need you to be careful, this place is too dangerous to be running around on your own! He then grabbed my arm very tightly, dragging me into the house and gave me a few strong whacks on my bottom and told my mother to keep me in the house. I sat there, somewhat destroyed.

My exploring had quickly come to an end. I knew I had to be back inside. I now had to watch out the window my father, Wayne and Drew working outside for a while. I asked my mother, "Can I go back outside?" She said, "You'll have to talk to your father." I went back out and told him that I wanted to help. He handed me a rake and said, "You can rake around all the buildings and throw any garbage into the trailer that's hooked up to the tractor." I had made it back outside. As I was raking, they were cleaning out all the buildings. They were throwing out all kinds of stuff. My brothers, of course, thought it was funny when they threw things on the ground where I had already raked. But I didn't care. I was helping and felt like part of the team. There were lots of interesting things they were bringing out of the buildings and setting outside. There was an old wood butter churn, a corn cob sheller that removed the kernels of corn from the corn cob. An old washboard for washing clothes. Lots of yard tools, picks, shovels, axes, sledgehammers and so on. I wanted to check out everything.

It was getting hot out, so my mom brought out one of my favorites, sweet, iced tea that she had made. It was so refreshing. We all drank down the tea and it was back to work. I felt so empowered that I was able to help. I had never been needed to help with anything before.

As I was raking around one of the buildings, I heard something inside. I didn't know what it was. I ran over and told my dad. He dropped what he was doing and slowly opened the door and started laughing. It was 4 chickens in the chicken coop. He hadn't even noticed that they were there. He walked in and seconds later came out with a handful of eggs! He handed me one telling me that they were very fragile. I held it very carefully. We took the eggs into the house and told my mom what I had found. She said, "Wow! That will be helpful with all these mouths to feed"! She washed them off and put them in the fridge. I was so proud! I felt like I was an asset to the family! Like I had struck gold! From that moment forward, I wanted to help more around the farm.

3

FALL

Age 2

As my dad called to wake us up as he did every morning in his usual way. "Boys! Get up! Time for breakfast!" As I opened my eyes, I could see my breath. It was cold! There was the smell of wood-burning and a light haze of smoke lingering in the air. There was a wood-burning stove located downstairs in the living room. It was the only source of heat in this two-story farmhouse. There had been an old coal-burning stove in the very small room in the cellar that the previous owner used to heat the house. Outside the side of the house was a couple of heavy wood doors that lifted to a coal shoot that led to the furnace in the cellar. There was a little coal leftover but not enough to use. My dad wanted nothing to do with the dirty coal furnace and decided to remove it. This made sense since we would have had to buy coal to burn. Using wood from our own forest would be so much cheaper. We had about one hundred and seventy-five acres of forested area that started at the top of a big hill about a hundred yards behind the farmhouse. It ran about a quarter of a mile deep and three-quarters of a mile long. All we had to do was cut enough and get it down to the house.

With the free labor, it was the cheapest alternative to heating such a big house, plus my dad had also set up a wood-burning stove to heat the shop area of the barn. There was a large pile of wood on the side of the barn that the old farm owner had previously cut before his unfortunate death. My dad believed that Olaf only used coal if he ran out of wood toward the end of the season. My dad being from the south, didn't realize how bad central Wisconsin winters could be. Even though there was a big pile, there wasn't enough to get through the entire winter. Once my dad saw how we were burning through so much wood every day, he took my older brothers and I up to the woods and started cutting more. They grabbed the chainsaws and axes, hooking up the trailer to the back of the tractor. We took that sandy trail that led out past the chicken coop, then along the end of the corn field and up the side of a big hill leading to the woods.

I followed along, walking behind. I was observing every plant, rock and bird along the way. I was back exploring my new surroundings. Once we were at the top of the hill, the path led by four straight rows of pine trees about twelve to fifteen feet tall. They all must have been planted at the same time. We drove a short way into the woods before finding a spot with some fallen trees. It was my job to stay back and pull branches as my dad cut them off with the chainsaw and pile them up for him. I was having the time of my life. There were so many trees surrounding me. I saw a few squirrels, lots of birds and even a red tail hawk. My brothers then picked up the big pieces and threw them into the trailer as I helped with small pieces I could handle. After a couple hours of hard work, we had the trailer loaded full of split wood. I had my first experience in the woods, and I couldn't wait to go back. It felt so natural, and I felt like there was so much to explore up there. We had barely gone into our woods, but it was a whole new world for me. The trail led even further back into the thick forest, and I wanted to know what it was like back there. My imagination raced with so many questions. What kind of animals and trees were deeper in the woods?

4

THE NEIGHBORS!

Age 3

I t was just after lunchtime, and I was hanging out in the front yard playing in the sand with my younger brother Lonnie when an old farm truck pulled into the driveway. It was a tall older man in overalls, work boots and a DeKalb Corn hat on. A small older lady got out of the passenger side. With a big smile, he asked if my dad was around. Just then, I heard my dad yelling, "Hey, Brett! What brings you by?"

Brett replied, "I was just checking in to see how things were going for you and your family." He added, "Sorry, it took so long to stop by, but it's been hard."

Brett was the younger brother of the previous owner, Olaf, who died in the car accident. Brett lived about a mile down our road on a dairy farm with his wife and son Gus, who is the same age as my brother Drew. Brett then introduced his wife, Cathy, to my dad. Then my mom came out of the house and met them both. Cathy had brought us an apple pie she had made to welcome us to the neighborhood. That caught my eye, and I was underfoot of my mom with anticipation to try the pie. Of course, we had to wait until after dinner to have it for dessert. It was well worth the wait! It was delicious. I don't think I've tasted any pie that good before. My mom rarely made us dessert. To us, dessert was a luxury. She would make a cake for our birthdays and banana pudding on occasion, but that was about it. My dad rarely ate sweets and one of his sayings was, "No one ever starved skipping dessert!" True, but I had a sweet tooth, and I would eat my buttered biscuit with jam on it for my dessert! I was always very thin, even though I ate enough for two kids my age. My dad would ask me if I had a hollow leg. We always worked hard every day on the farm. We were growing boys, so we had big appetites and I always made sure to eat my share at meals and I never left the table hungry.

5

STRANGER IN THE WOODS

Age 4

It was a sunny but chilly evening toward the beginning of November. I had just turned 4 years old. My mom made my favorite for dinner. Fried chicken, mashed potatoes and gravy. Then we had birthday cake, and I opened my present of a new shirt. Our presents were almost always a practical gift of a new shirt, pants, socks or underwear. After helping Mom clear the table, all I knew was what I wanted to do next. Go see the horses. They loved it when I would come to visit them.

I would always throw some hay and corn in their feeding trough. As I was hanging out petting the horses in their shed toward the back of the farm, I heard a weird noise coming from the corner of the woods by the pine trees. It sounded like a deep gruff grunt. The horses immediately started to become uneasy and were now nervously pacing in their stalls. Their eyes were bugging out and they were definitely frightened. Something has them extremely spooked!

I didn't see anything as I turned toward the woods where the noise had come from. There was a reddish glow from the setting sun that was shining on the hillside and the edge of the woods. I started to head back toward the house when I heard a tree branch snap from the same area where I had heard the grunt. Then about one hundred yards away, I saw a very tall dark figure walk between the trees. I could tell that he was looking toward me as he walked but was only visible about one second. He was wearing all dark clothing from top to bottom. I thought it might have been a neighbor of ours. It was hard to see. Our neighbor's property was just on the other side of the fence line. I really didn't think too much of it. I walked into the hayloft of the barn and started climbing the hay bales. They were stacked up about twenty feet high. My older brothers had built a maze in the stacks of bails. I started crawling through the tunnels they had made. It was a lot of fun. After a little fun, I heard my dad whistle to come in because it was getting dark out. I washed up and my dad asked what I was up to outside. I told him I was petting the horses and that I saw the neighbor by the edge of the woods. He said, "That would have been Tim on the east side of our property." I said, "He was really a tall guy." I added, "I think he was wearing a ten-gallon hat. Like what some cowboys would wear in old western TV shows." My dad laughed and that was the end of the conversation.

A few days later, my dad and I ran into Tim in town at the General Store and asked if he or anyone was up in the woods. He said, "I haven't been in the wood in years due to my bad knee." He also said, "No one should have been up there. However, there is a snowmobile trail that runs along the fence line, but we had no snow yet." My dad then asked, "Do you know if anyone around here that wears a cowboy hat?"

Tim laughed and said, "This isn't Texas, Aubrey." They both then laughed. My dad then questioned me on the way back home. Basically, about if I really saw this guy. I said yes and he said, "Well, if you see anyone again, let me know". He said there's a possibility of some hunters and he thought they might be hunting illegally on our land or the neighbors land. So, to be careful.

I spent the next few days keeping an eye out for any unwanted guests. There was nothing to report and I soon forgot about it.

6

THE SHOP

Age 4

After many long hard days of cleanup on the farm, my dad was now able to start working on a business idea he had. It was a snowy December day, and the bottom floor of the barn was now being converted into a workshop.

We were going to have to clean it out completely and seal it up against the long Wisconsin winters. What a job that was going to be. This was a milk house barn with manure gutters and lots of old milk machines that were hooked up to an air system that would suck the milk from the udders of each cow. There were metal stations that would gently lock the cow's head into it while it was being milked. My dad and brothers basically had to gut the place. They then had to insulate it and put-up plywood walls.

My dad's business adventure was starting up a furniture and auto upholstery business. It was the perfect time to do so since we wouldn't be able to plant any crops in the fields until next spring. Since my dad was a parachute rigger for twenty-two years in the Army and Navy, he knew how to use a sewing machine. Not just your mom's little sewing machine for making clothes, but he purchased a

Singer sewing machine that could sew heavy-duty truck tarps even if needed. It was four times the size of a normal household sewing machine. That was the beginning of Aubrey & Sons Upholstery.

My dad showed my two older brothers how to take apart furniture and car seats. Then he had my mom cut apart all the material at the original sewing seams. She would then use the old material pieces as a pattern for the new piece by tracing around them onto the new material. She would then cut these new pieces out and my dad would then sew them together. After being sewn, they would be ready to be put back on the furniture. Once trained by my dad, Drew did mostly the furniture and Wayne did the auto upholstery. At four years old, I was too young to help much with the business. I wanted to help so much. I asked my dad, "When can I learn to help?" My dad replied, "Maybe when you turn five." I was feeling bummed and a little left out at the time. Even though my older brothers didn't want me hanging around much, I did so as much as possible. I've always felt if you could show me how to do something, I would be willing to try and do it. A classic case of I want to do what you're doing! I had in my mind that in one year, I would be able to do everything my older brothers were doing!

7

HOME LIFE

Age 4

Since the school year started, my two older brothers went to grade school in town during the week. I was jealous! I wanted to go to school too! I only had one year to wait before kindergarten. Before they would go, they had to feed and water all the animals on the farm. Usually, it took about fifteen minutes. My dad would eat breakfast and head out to the shop and work on the upholstery business. Recovering chairs, couches, bar stool seats, car seats and the list goes on. Anything that had material on it, he would recover it with new material. It was surprisingly a good start for the business being way out in the backwoods. He advertised in local newspapers in neighboring towns and would advertise free estimates, free pickup and delivery. My dad would take a break for lunch and then usually he would then take about an hour nap and then back to work till about 5pm.

My mom would help him lift some of the heavier furniture and cut out the patterns of the new material to be sewed. She did most of the work in the house so she could watch Lonnie and me. She always started her day making breakfast for us boys. Then laundry, cleaning the house, making lunch, dinner and of course all those dishes! She always tended to us boys' need every day! This is on top of the fact that she was also pregnant with my baby brother Dean.

My mom was the opposite of my dad. He was stern, loud, short-tempered and liked to have his beer and whiskey and was a chain smoker of his Paul Malls. My mom was quiet, soft-spoken, calm and didn't drink alcohol or smoke. They were total opposites. The worst thing my mom would say when she felt frustrated was, "For Pete's sake!" She was a saint! She would never think of using foul language.

Once my brothers got back home from school, they would again feed and water the animals. Then my dad would have them help around the shop. They would carry wood into the shop and house for the fireplace, shovel snow, sweep the shop and take out the garbage. Drew was learning to do the furniture and Wayne was learning the auto seats part of the upholstery business. They had learned how to take apart the furniture, but now my dad was teaching them both to put the new materials back on. Not an easy task. I would follow my brothers around as they did their chores, trying to help by filling the animal troughs with water, carrying small pieces of wood, holding the dustpan as they swept etc... I was always watching and learning so that I could help more around the shop.

Saturdays were the day that my mom would go grocery shopping in Portage, a small town about twenty-five minutes away. It was much bigger than Briggsville. I always wanted to go with. It was one on one time with mom, which was always enjoyable. Also, as any little boy, I would try to get her to buy me some of my favorite foods and, of course, some candy. It was so exciting to see all the different foods available. I was always asking her, "What is that?" Being so secluded on the farm all day, we didn't see very many people. So, seeing people and all the hustle and bustle of the city was always enjoyable. Very different from the farm life. We would sometimes have to stop at the feed mill for supplies for the animals and, at times, the hardware store. I really liked going there. They had all kinds of cool equipment and tools. I wanted them all! I found going into these businesses very exciting. These trips were expanding my world and I wanted to explore it all! I wanted to know what was going on in all the buildings in town. My mom's favorite thing to say to me was, "No!"

On this day, as we were driving up the road we lived on, my mom suddenly hit the brakes. The groceries in the back of the van came tumbling toward the front, spilling out all over the floor. I was startled and my mom bleated out, "What the heck was that?" As she said that, I saw something big and dark running away through the thick brush, heading deeper into the woods. As my mom continued driving by, I caught a glimpse of what looked like a guy running quickly up the hillside into Tim's woods. It was on two legs, but I couldn't really see through all the thick foliage. I said, "I think it's that guy that I saw earlier!"

My mom angrily replied, "He must be looking to get run over!"

After getting all the groceries picked up and into the house, my mom told my dad about the guy. She told him that she had seen him dart across the road and then into the ditch and off into the woods. She then said, "He must have a death wish!" My dad asked me, "Did you see him?" I replied, "Yep! It's that hermit guy!"

My dad said to my mom, "Next time, just run him over!"

My mom scoffed and mumbled, "That's all we need."

8

WINTER

Age 4

Now that winter was here, we were waking up every day to the smell of wood-burning and, of course, my mom cooking breakfast. Today was going to be a little different. My dad announced that he would be taking my brothers and me sledding. It was snowing and there was a new layer of fluffy white snow on the ground making for excellent sledding weather. To top it all off, we didn't have to go far. There was a large hill about one hundred yards long that led to the woods. When we lived in the city the winter before, we had a small hill next to our house that was only about fifteen feet long. I had thought that was fun. This was going to be great. We got on our snow pants, winter jackets, stocking hats, long socks and to keep our feet dry, my mom always saves bread bags. We put those on over our socks and then our boots over the bag. The bags would make it easy to put on our boots and, they would keep our feet dry and warm. We were ready to go! We grabbed our sleds and we all headed up the big hill.

The hill was so big it would take about five minutes or more to drag the sleds up to the top. Once we got to the top, Wayne and Drew immediately jumped on one sled together and took off. They were laughing as they went flying down the hill. I was ready to go as well, but my younger brother Lonnie was scared and didn't want to go. Once my two older brothers were back up top, my dad said, "Watch Lonnie until we get back up here." My dad had me sit on the front of the sled and he sat on the back. He put both feet around me and then onto the steering. He asked, "Are you ready?" I said, "Yes!" with great anticipation. Then he asked Wayne to give us a push. Off we went! We picked up speed and it was a little bumpy. About halfway down the hill, we were going so fast that I knew if we wrecked, it was going to hurt. We made it all the way down without wiping out. It was the most fun I think I had ever had. I couldn't stop smiling. We ran back up the hill as fast as we could for another run. Lonnie still didn't want to go down, so my dad walked him back to the house. The next time I went down with Wayne and then with Drew once. They showed me how to steer the sled and I went down all by myself. I must admit I was a little scared the first time sledding by myself. Wayne gave me a big push. I went flying down that hill. It was so exhilarating. I felt very confident and didn't need to go on a sled with anyone anymore.

As we were at the top of the hill catching our breath, we suddenly smelled something terrible. It was so bad we were gagging. It smelled like rotting roadkill. Wayne said, "Oh my God! Something is dead around here!" The wind was blowing from the woods, but we couldn't see anything. As we were about to jump on the sleds again, we then heard my dad whistle for us to come back inside. We sled back down and ran to the house. As we opened the door, out came warmth and the smell of one of my favorites grilled peanut butter and jelly sandwiches! It was like having dessert for lunch. All is good! Winter was a lot of fun too.

9

THE CROPS

Age 4

It was now spring, and we had made it through with our first winter. We burned all the wood we had cut and in order to make it through the rest of the winter, we had to cut down a couple trees near the farm due to the snow was too deep to get into the woods. The temperature was rising, and all the trees and grass were all turning green again. I couldn't wait to explore more of the farm with my older brothers. As usual, they didn't want me to tag along, but I did anyway! They picked on me and always told me to go back to the house. I was never deterred and followed anyway from a distance.

My mom had brought my new little brother Dean into the world a couple weeks ago and she was spending most of her time taking care of him. There were now five boys. Her life, as busy as it was, just got even busier. She now relied on my older brothers to watch me more. They were not thrilled about me tagging along and complained about it all the time. Sometimes they would try to be funny and take off running as fast as they could to try and lose me. I would try to keep up, but I couldn't and would just wait them out. They would eventually have to show back up at the house.

It is now the time of year for my dad to get the crops started. There is a lot of work involved in planting crops. My dad sat me on the edge of the field under a big apple tree so I could watch him plow and till the soil in the field. I saw how he turned the soil over with the plow in nice rows. Then he used a disc behind the tractor to break the rows into smaller, smoother soil. After a whole day of working the soil, he then brought out a flat hay wagon behind the tractor. He had my older brothers and I pick up any rocks for the next couple of days. It was dirty, hard work. We had to follow along as my dad drove back and forth across the field and loaded all the rocks we could find onto the wagon. Then unload the big ones in a pile and the small stones we used to solidify our dirt driveway.

It felt so good to run around the field barefoot in the soft soil. I again felt like I was part of the team. Now my dad was ready to plant our first crop of corn. He hooked up the planter to the back of the tractor and filled the planter with corn seed. The planter dropped seeds into little holes in nice, neat rows and then a blade would cover them up with dirt. After he was done, my father stood back with a tear in his eye and admired his work. He patted me on the head and then said, "Now all we need is rain!" My goofy older brothers danced around as if they were doing a native rain dance. We all laughed and thought maybe it would work, so I joined in.

I went out the next day and nothing had grown yet. It rained hard the third day. I went out the fourth and fifth day and still nothing. I thought maybe we didn't do it right. My dad said, "Give it time." So, on the eighth day, there were all these little green sprouts of corn growing all over the field. I ran into the shop and started yelling to my dad. "They're growing, they're growing!" He walked out with my brothers and me in tow to check it out. He then said, "You keep an eye on them." I was glad to do so. I now had a responsibility. I checked them nearly every day! About three days later, I went to check the corn again and along the edge of the trail heading toward the woods were a few large barefoot impressions toward the old apple tree. I ran and told my dad and he said, "This hermit guy better stay off our property." So, the next day we went into Briggsville and stopped by the General Store. My dad grabbed several "No Trespassing" signs that he put up all around our property. My dad then laughed and said, "I hope this guy can read!"

Around the beginning of July, our neighbor Brett stopped by checking on us and told me, "There is an old saying for corn. You're on track if your corn is knee-high by the 4th. of July!" I replied, "I guess we are ahead of that since the corn comes to my chest." Brett laughed and then clarified, "I was referring to an adults' knee." I laughed with him knowing how silly I was!

10

FIREWORKS

Age 4

It was the 4th. of July and we were all headed to Briggsville for the parade. As we drove into town, there were lots of parked cars that lined down the street. People were streaming from their cars toward the small Veterans Park located in the center of town. Most were wearing red, white and blue clothing and were all talking to each other. There was excitement in the air!

There was ice cream, popcorn, cotton candy vendors. In the center was the VFW tent that on one side was serving hamburgers, brats and hotdogs and on the other was the beer tent. That's where most of the men and my dad were. There were children hanging around a clown making all sorts of animal balloons. My mom took all of us boys to an open picnic table and came back with hamburgers for all of us. It was the first time that I remembered eating something my mom hadn't cooked. It was soooo good! About then, we could hear off in the distance were the sound of drums beating. The parade was about to start.

First up was the Dells High School marching band. Marching right down the street. Everyone's attention was now on the parade.

Next up was a fire truck with firemen waving and the blaring of its siren. The firemen riding was also throwing out candy to the kids. The kids scrambled to pick it up before the others. I was able to grab a few pieces. Then there were several really old cars. There was an A Model, a Corvette, a Thunderbird and a 57 Chevy. Then a few old trucks followed by some old tractors. Then they had an amphibious all-terrain vehicle that was from World War II with several old military veterans waving. They called the vehicle a "Duck" because it could drive on land but also floated in the water. They were made famous from the D Day invasion of Normandy, France, during World War II. There's a tourist river ride in the Dells that used several of these for tours of the Wisconsin River. The Dells is a town about twenty minutes west where we all would later go to Jr. high and high school. Next came a brand-new green John Deer tractor with four huge tires on the back and a cab the driver sat in. I couldn't believe how big it was. It was several times the size of our tractor. Then we see the Zor Shrine driving these little go-cart-sized cars in figure eights. They were beeping their horns the whole time. They were quite silly and entertaining. Then there was a hay wagon float with the US flag and uniformed soldiers waving and throwing out more candy! Everyone stood and my dad even saluted as they went by. The last was the local sheriffs blaring his siren and, on the loudspeaker, wishing everyone a happy 4th of July.

Once the parade was over, a small band started performing at the gazebo in the center of the park. My mom and Wayne went over to the ice cream stand and brought back an ice cream cone for each of us. It was rare for us to have treats or even dessert after dinner. So, this was truly a special day! While we ate our ice cream, I noticed a bunch of kids were going swimming across the street in the lake. My mom took us over and walked in the water with us. I had never been swimming before. Wayne and Drew dove right in. My mom sat by the edge with her feet in the water with Lonnie and Dean in her arms. As I slowly walked in, I noticed the bottom was a little slimy. I continued going deeper until the water was up to my chin. I could feel my body starting to float. My mom then said I was too deep, and I made my way in a little shallower. Of course, my older brothers decided to splash me so much that I felt like I couldn't breathe. I wanted to swim all day! Then my dad came over and said it was time to go. My mom then gathered us all up and we made our way back to the car. I think that was the best day of my life so far. I wanted every day to be just like that! Little did I know there was to be more to celebrate. Shortly after dinner, it was beginning to get dark out. Then we heard this loud boom in the distance. We could hear a lot out there in the country due to not very many people living near us. My dad said, "Looks like it's starting!"

My dad had everyone go outside and climb on top of a horse shelter that was just across the street overlooking the open fields. We could see the lake in Briggsville about two miles away as the crow flies. Then we see a rocket shoot up in the air from near the lake and explode with a loud boom! The boom took about ten seconds to reach us. It was my 1st fireworks. They were all kinds of colors of red, white, blue, green. The fireworks lasted about half an hour. I was in awe! That was absolutely the best time we had as a family.

11

FIREWOOD

Age 4

I t was an early August morning and I was in the woods cutting up dead trees that lay all over the forest floor with my two older brothers. My job was to pick up the little sticks and pull any branches away. We were able to load the truck and the trailer full of cut wood by lunchtime. We unloaded and stacked both at the end of the barn. After lunch, we were sent back up to get another load. We were going to work our way down the trail further into the woods. We were driving just past where we had worked earlier that day when Wayne hit the brakes and we saw a tree blocking the trail. We got out and both of my brothers thought that was weird. This was a live green tree about 8 inches in diameter. The roots were ripped out of the ground and weren't there this morning. There was no wind and why was that the only live tree that had fallen. So Wayne said, "Whatever, let's cut it up too"! So, he got out the chainsaw and we cut it up and loaded it. Then we moved about another twenty-five yards further into the woods. As we were parking the truck, I saw something big dash across the trail about fifty yards away. It was so fast. I said, "I think I just saw a deer." My brothers joked and said, "Don't let it eat you". I wasn't afraid of deer. I had seen them many times driving and down in the field. My dad already told us about all the animals that live around here. He said they don't attack humans. Even a black bear or a cougar would normally stay away from humans. The main thing he said was don't corner them. Then they can become defensive. Especially be careful if any animal has babies around. The mother will do whatever it takes to protect their young. I wanted to go find the deer, but we had work to do.

We continued to cut and load the truck and trailer till we filled them. It was getting late by the time we finished unloading, splitting and stacking all the wood. Our mom called us in for dinner just as we were finishing. It was another one of my favorites! Swiss steak, slow-cooked steak in a sweet Italian tomato sauce with mashed potatoes and corn! We always had biscuits for dinner. Afterward, I decided to go lay on top of the garage and look at the stars. I would turn out the yard light and just be in awe of how many stars I could see. I could see the Milky Way. Every now and then, I could see shooting stars zipping across the sky. It made me feel like such a small piece of the universe. I lay there thinking of what it would be like to be an astronaut and visit the moon. I loved watching the show, *Flash Gordon*. I wondered if there was alien life out there. As I lay there, I started hearing what sounded like someone chopping wood. It wasn't coming from the farm area. I stood up to listen. It seemed to be coming from the woods near the east fence line area. I couldn't see any lights, but it's possible that the neighbors were up there. Just thought it was late and a weird time to be cutting wood. I only heard it a couple times more. It echoed through the woods. I didn't see any lights or hear any trucks or tractors leave the area. So I went back to my stargazing until my mom called me in for bed. I lay there for a few minutes, wondering what tomorrow was going to bring.

12

SCHOOL

Age 5

I was five years old now and I was excited for my first day of kindergarten. I got up with my two older brothers and helped feed and water the animals. Then a quick breakfast and wait at the end of the driveway for the bus to pick us up. We could hear it coming a mile away. It stopped at the farms down the road with its flashing red lights. It then stopped for us. Wayne and Drew got on the bus, and I followed. There were about eight kids already that lived further out. Wayne and Drew sat in the back and I sat in front of them in an open seat. We picked up about a dozen more kids of all ages before reaching the Briggsville grade school. I was a little nervous as we got off. My brothers jumped off and headed to their classrooms since they went there the year before. As I got off, a lady asked who I was. I told her, and she had me line up in the hall with some others. Then she came and said, "Follow me."

She led all ten of us into the kindergarten classroom. I had never really been around other kids before. It was a new experience, and I had sensory overload. We were assigned a desk and went around the room, introducing who we were. There was a very pretty girl that smiled at me as she stood up and told us who she was. Her name was Lisa. I had a hard time taking my eyes off her. After everyone introduced themselves, we started working on our ABCs. I felt a little dumb when some of the students already knew what they were. I had never been taught anything other than farm life. We didn't even have coloring books or crayons as kids. It was a tough start for my first day of school. There was a little snack break, and they gave us white or chocolate milk. I chose chocolate. I had never had chocolate milk before. It was so much better than white milk. We only went half a day while 1st grade and up went full days. At noon a small bus took us, the kindergarten kids, back home. There were only five of us on that bus. The rest of the kids lived in town and were dropped off and picked up by their parents. That's when I started to talk to a couple of the kids. Liam who lived on a dairy farm about a mile away and Thad, whose dad was a mason or bricklayer. I had made my first friends.

Once I returned home, my mom asked, "How was your first day of school?" I said, "Good, I made friends and started learning my ABCs." Then I gave her a list that we needed for class. Crayons, glue, pencils and a mat for us to take a nap on. I then mentioned I had chocolate milk and how good it was. My dad overheard and said, "What is this world coming to?" He thought that having chocolate milk was spoiling the kids.

School was going great. I was eager to be there every day. I was able to talk and have friends that were my own age. I quickly learned my studies. I really enjoyed learning about so many things. Kindergarten went so well that the teacher had me go out in the hall a couple times and work with a couple other students that weren't faring as well. I realized that I also liked helping others as well.

13

PREDATOR

Age 5

It was a cold, late November day. Now that I was five years old, I had been doing my normal rounds of feeding and watering all the animals. I had to throw slop to the pigs. Slop was any food scraps we didn't eat or couldn't eat. Then we put corn and hay in for the cows, ground corn for the chickens and corn and a special feed for the horses. I would usually spend more time with the horses. I loved petting and brushing them. You could tell they loved the attention. Anytime I went near the animals, they would all get so excited, knowing that it was time to eat. Pretty much the same as my brothers and I did. We would race to the dinner table. My dad would always be yelling for us to slow down, don't slam the door and so on.

Then just before we were called in for dinner, I was helping shovel a little snow off the driveway down by the road when I saw something just east of the farm dart across the road about seventy-five yards away along the fence line. I yelled out, "What is that? It looks like a huge dog." It must have heard me. It stopped and looked at us for a minute, checking us out. My dad heard the commotion and grabbed his binoculars and said, "It's a wolf." We took turns watching it saunter along the edge of the field, getting further away. I wasn't scared but knew this was something I should respect and didn't want to meet face to face.

My dad returned to the house and called our local Sheriff, Ted Ware. He was the only law enforcement in our area. Ted then reported the sighting to the DNR. It was a couple weeks later when a green truck pulled up with a large box on the back. A couple guys in green uniforms get out and ask for my dad. I ran inside quickly and got him. When we came out, they had the back of the box opened and hauled out a large cage with a cover over it. They took the cover off and to my shock, was a huge growling wolf. I stepped behind my dad a little as he said, "I'll be damned, you caught it!" Instantly the dogs went crazy! This thing looked fierce! Its teeth were huge! It was twice as big as our German Shepard, Smokey. They said they had trapped it after it had attacked a neighbor's dog. It was a Timberwolf. I was glad this was no longer roaming free around the farm and a threat to the livestock and not to mention us. The DNR Guys said that it was a lone wolf and that there shouldn't be any others around but to always keep our eyes open. Especially when in the woods. From that point on, my dad said we should always have a gun with us when cutting wood up in the woods. He told me to never go near the woods or too far from the house alone.

14

BASEBALL

Age 5

I t was our first weekend off school and my dad and I went on a business call to pick up some furniture and to do an estimate at another. As we were heading home my dad did his usual and stopped by a tavern to have a few drinks. We stopped at The Mill Inn in Briggsville. I didn't mind because my dad would buy me a soda and talk to me a little more than usual. He would tell whoever would listen stories from all his life and military experience. And he had lots of them. We were just sitting there when a guy in a ball cap came in wanting a can of soda. The bartender says, "What's going on today, Larry?"

Larry replied, "We are holding a Little League tryout over at the baseball diamond." He then looks at me and says, "How old are you, kid?"

I responded, "Five."

He said, "Perfect."

As he approaches us, he says, "You're a big strapping kid." Then asked, "Have you ever played baseball before?"

"I've played catch several times with my brothers."

He says to my dad, "You should get this boy over to the park right away."

My dad said, "Ok," and told Larry, "I'll bring him right over."

Larry said, "Great! I'll see you over there." My dad grabs a twelve-pack of beer to go, and we head over to the ball diamond. I was excited but also very nervous. I played a lot with my brothers, but not anything ever organized.

Right away, Larry (Coach) talked to about fifteen of us about seeing what positions we would be best at. There were even two girls that were playing. I didn't think twice about having them there. We all started out playing catch and loosening our arms up. I was taller than all the kids. We then all lined up and took grounders and throwing over to 1st base. This was what I was used to so far. Then we went to the outfield and took fly balls and throwing into 2nd base. I would throw the ball as high as I could at home and catch them. But Coach was hitting these were really high. It took a few to catch on, but I did ok. Then, Coach had us take batting practice. I had never done that before. He called me up to the plate after a few others had their ten swings. He tossed the ball and I swung and missed. I was embarrassed because everyone was looking. Then I heard my dad's voice saying, "Keep your eye on the ball! Watch it all the way till you hit it off the bat." The next one, I fouled off to the backstop. I felt a lot more confident. On the next pitch, I hit to the shortstop. Then I hit it hard over 3rd base. Then to centerfield a couple times and left a couple more. My dad yells out! "That's my boy". No one else hit the ball as far! A couple kids didn't even hit the ball. Coach handed all the kids a schedule and said we all made the team. He walked over to my dad and said, "We would love for him to play on the team." My dad said, "Just as long as he gets all his work done!" Coach patted me on the back and said, "Welcome to the team kid." I was very excited! I couldn't wait to go home and tell mom all about it.

15

THE BLIZZARD OF THE CENTURY

Age 5

I was enjoying another day of school when the teacher had a visit from the school secretary. She seemed a little flustered and their conversation was very serious. The teacher then announced that we would be cutting the day short due to a major snowstorm was headed our way. We were connected to the Wis. Dells school district where the Jr. High and High School were located. They were just twelve miles west and were already getting heavy snow and sent the kids home. There was a nervous excitement in the air with the storm approaching. The skies were getting very dark, and cars were driving by had their lights on. Once the bus pulled up, it was starting to snow heavily. We left the school and headed home. It took about 30 minutes to get back due to the very slippery roads. Since the school had called and informed them we were coming home early, my mom had lunch ready for us all. My dad thought this was crazy and told us again the story of how he walked 3 miles uphill both ways to and from school every day in the heat of central Alabama. We already have heard that story several times.

We already had a few feet of snow built up on the ground over the winter. The tractor with a scoop bucket is what we used to plow our driveway whenever it snowed hard. If it was light snow of six inches or less, we would shovel it by hand. Even my younger brother Lonnie was now able to help a little.

We ate our lunch, and it was getting darker out. It was snowing so hard that our yard light turned on. The yard light is just like a city streetlight. We had one next to the house with a light sensor on it. It would turn on at sunset to light up the driveway. It was about 1 PM and the snow was coming down so hard now that I almost couldn't see the barn. I loved to be outside and especially when it was snowing. So, my brothers and I all got dressed and had a snowball fight. My mom said, "Make sure you stay where I can see you!" After a few minutes, Lonnie didn't like how rough our older brothers could get, so he ran back inside. The snow was really piling up. There were now about six inches. I had enough, so I went inside as well to warm up. My older brothers went out to the shop to help dad with upholstery work.

After dinner, it was still snowing, so my dad plowed about fifteen inches of snow out of the driveway and around all the farm buildings so we could get to the animals in the morning. He put extra hay in all the animal shelters and closed all the doors as we did at night to help keep them warm. When we were heading to bed, it was still snowing hard. You could hear the wind whistling by the windows. As I was falling asleep, I looked out the bedroom window, but I couldn't even see the big oak tree that was twenty feet away.

We woke up the next morning thinking we were going to school. It was cold in the house. As we came hurtling down the stairs, my mom shouted, "No school today!" I asked, "Why not?" She said, "Have you looked outside?" I ran to the window, but it was covered in frost. I used my fingernails and scraped off enough to peek through and saw we had gotten another two feet of snow, but the worst part was the temperature and the wind. It was 20° below zero with 60° below zero wind chills. The wind had also blown snowdrifts as high as the roofline of the house and about ten-to-fifteen-foot drifts around all the buildings. I wanted to go see, but my mom said, "You stay here." I tried to look outside, but snow and frost were covering the windows.

My dad was outside trying to get the tractor started, so he could plow the driveway. It was so cold that my dad had to take the battery off and bring it into the house to warm up for a while. After eating breakfast, he put the battery back on and the tractor reluctantly started. My dad had to start all over. It was as if he hadn't plowed the snow the night before. It took a few hours to get access to all the buildings and the driveway clear. Then we had to really bundle up to feed and water the animals. As soon as I walked outside, the cold wind took my breath away. I quickly put my scarf over my face and only had an opening for my eyes. I even could feel the cold hitting my eyes. We had heating elements that we used to keep their water troughs from totally freezing up. We took a couple pictures of all the snow and the snowdrifts. We had to do our chores as quickly as possible. Our farm life pretty much went on as normal, but we were on the outside edge of our County. As far as you could get from the county's snowplows. It took three days for snowplows to get through all the drifts and snow. We missed a total of three- and one-half days of school. The kids that lived in town only missed one and a half days.

Several of the farmers used their tractors to help the snowplows that couldn't get through. Because some of the snowdrifts were so big, the snowplows were even getting stuck. The neighbors all checked on each other, seeing if anyone needed help. My brothers and I helped a couple neighbors shovel out their driveways and buildings. It was fun helping and they gave us treats and twenty-five cents. I had money for the first time!

16

FIRE!

Age 5

It's now mid-summer and life on the farm was picking up for me. The upholstery business was growing rapidly for my dad, my older brothers and me. There are many small duties in the shop that I would help with almost on a daily basis. Besides sweeping up the floors and hauling out garbage, my dad had me taking tacks and staples that held on the material out of small furniture like bar stools, kitchen chairs and footstools. It was hard work because furniture at the time was made from hard oak. Pulling out the tacks and staples was sometimes nearly impossible for me. I did what I could and left the rest for my stronger, older brothers.

When I wasn't helping in the shop, my job was to help my mom pull weeds in the garden. My mom had all kinds of vegetables planted, from tomatoes, green beans, cucumbers, lettuce, green onions to potatoes, sweet corn, popcorn and my favorite fruits like watermelon, strawberries and grapes. Heck, we even grew peanuts. They grew underground just like a potato. I enjoyed the time spent with mom helping in the garden. She was always teaching me how they grew, how to care for them and when they were ripe for picking.

She was in her element out there. As she pulled weeds from around the plants, she would hum a tune she liked. I think that the garden was where she found peace and quiet from all of us boys.

It was a hot Sunday evening. After a long day working, we sat down for dinner. It, of course, included some of our fresh veggies from the garden. Tonight, we had green beans and baked potatoes that mom and I picked earlier. Afterward, we all relaxed and watched one of my favorite movies from *The Wonderful World of Disney* on TV. These movies came on every Sunday night during the summer. It was really our only time that we all sat together as a family other than meals. The rest of the time, we had our chores and duties to get done.

Once the movie was over, we all hit the sack. We all worked hard on the farm. Even at five years old, I was putting in a full day's work and then some. We really didn't have a lot of time to be kids and play. We didn't even have many toys. So, once I put my head on the pillow, it was always lights out. I would wake up usually to the voice of my dad yelling, "Time to get up! Breakfast is ready!" But not this night. I woke up to my dad yelling, "Fire! The barn is on Fire! Everyone get up and get dressed quickly!" We all jumped up and dressed in just a few seconds. You could smell the smoke and the night sky was lit up with an orange glow, almost like daytime. We ran downstairs and saw, to our horror, the barn partially engulfed in flames. We were all in shock. My dad told Lonnie and I to stay with mom under a tree by the house. My dad and two older brothers were trying to spray a garden hose on the fire and scooping buckets of water out of a horse trough and dousing the barn with no effect. I could hear a fire engine's siren in the distance getting closer. By the time the only fire engine from Briggsville reached us, the whole barn was now on fire. The flames were reaching seventy feet above the barn. We were across the driveway, and we had to move back to the front yard due to the leaves on the tree we were sitting under were starting to smoke and the heat was unbearable. The fireman did all they could to stop the fire to no prevail. My dad sat underneath the tree that we were under earlier with tears in his eyes and his hands over his face repeated over and over, "What are we going to do now? What are we going to do now?"

The upholstery shop was in the bottom of the barn, along with several customers' furniture. The hayloft was half full of hay and we wouldn't have any more until the crops were harvested in the fall.

After a few more hours of dousing the fire until it was completely out, the firemen finally left. The fire had destroyed the barn completely. The next day several of our neighbors showed up with corn and hey in the back of their trucks and wagons. Some of the wives brought food and baked goods for us to eat. The outpouring was so wonderful for everyone. A real sense of community and compassion.

The fire inspector came out early the next morning and after going through the debris, they told me that there was old faulty wiring that started the fire. He also mentioned that it must have woke the neighbors to the east of us. That two of the firemen reported someone standing at the edge of the woods watching as they put the fire out. My dad told the inspector that that must of been the Hermit guy. The inspector smiled and said, "What?" My dad told him "There is some guy living in the neighbor's woods somewhere." The inspector shrugged it off and left.

We lost everything in the shop. All the sewing machines, all the tools and most of all the customers' pieces of furniture that we were working on. The insurance company covered the tools and all but not the customers' furniture. Luckily my dad was taking Polaroid pictures of before and after for a scrapbook that he could show customers. My dad sent my mom and I to several auctions and yard sales to try and replace all that was lost.

I really enjoyed hanging out with my mom. She was always kind, and we could actually have conversations, unlike my dad. My dad was more like our boss than what I guess a normal father would be like. It took my mom and me awhile, but we eventually replaced all the lost furniture. Some we were able to replace exactly the same and some we had to settle but were close to the original. The customers ended up all to be very understanding and happy!

In the meantime, my dad and older brothers cleared the way in the living room of the farmhouse for an area where we could do the upholstery shop. It was going to be tight. We used the dining room table during the day to work on furniture. My dad replaced everything with all new tools, air compressor, staple guns and so on. We had no choice but to have work and home in the farmhouse together for about a year. My dad was very stressed, and he was starting to drink more. He yelled at us kids more and my mom was becoming frustrated with the whole situation. She wished we had never left the city.

17

FOOTPRINTS

Age 6

It was finally Spring again and each day was now beginning to get slightly longer. During the winter, we would get up to do our daily morning chores when it was dark and get back from school with the sun setting within an hour. We had to hustle to feed and water the animals, shovel any snow and get wood for the house before dark. Wayne and Drew mostly worked with my dad after school. I helped out as much as I could. I really didn't like winter very much. Sledding and all was fun, but winter was kind of dark depressing and kept us inside the house. I preferred to be outside where I could explore, and everything was alive.

The temperatures were warming up slightly and nearly all that snow we had this winter melted and since there was so much, the field across the street had flooded at the bottom. It looked like a lake. After lunch, my dad took his usual nap. My older brothers and I went to investigate the body of water. The field was a little muddy, but as we got closer, it was too muddy to continue. I was losing my boots in the thick, sticky mud. So, we headed for a row of several large hickory nut trees that had better ground to walk on. There was still a little snow under them that hadn't melted yet. We could see deer tracks all over and then I saw what looked like a very large human footprint. You could see the toes and it was pretty deep. My brother Drew, who now was almost six feet tall and had size twelve shoes, put his boot next to it and we were surprised when his boot print was still about four inches smaller and a couple inches narrower than the barefoot track. My oldest brother Wayne then said, "Who would be out here barefoot in this weather?" The high temp is only about 45° out." There were several other tracks, but they weren't defined like this one. I thought back about the stranger I had seen before along the edge of our woods. Maybe it was him. He was a really big guy! I had a hard time believing he would be out here barefoot.

We made our way back to the house and my brothers told my dad about the footprints. He shrugged it off and said, "That's not our property across the street anyway. Brett owns it." Then said, "We can use it for grazing our cows and horses during the warmer months since he wasn't using the land at the time." The land had belonged to his brother, the old farm owner, but Brett kept the fields across the street when he sold us the farm. Our dad then reminded us we had work to do. We washed our boots off with the hose and went back to work. As I was sweeping the shop floor, I couldn't help but think about the footprints. After I was done sweeping, I went outside to see how it would feel to walk in the snow and mud barefoot. So, I took off one of my shoes and sock. Then stood up and took a few steps. Within ten seconds, I couldn't stand the pain. I quickly put my sock and shoe back on and ran back into the house. I told my mom what I had done. She said, "You did what?" I told her about the footprints across the street in the field. She said, "Well, that doesn't mean you should do it!"

I said, "It's way too cold to be running around outside barefoot. I don't know how that guy does it!"

She asked, "What guy?"

"The guy who lives in the woods."

She then said, "Oh, the guy I almost ran over?" Then she finished with, "He better not be living in our woods!"

18

THE NEW HOUSE

Age 6

Living and working in the same space over the last year was really rough on the whole family. We literally would remove our work from the dining room table to eat and then clear it to return the work project at the time. I remember times when we may not have swept well enough the night before and waking up to stepping on a tack or staple on our way to the bathroom. Quite the wake-up call! That was all about to change! With the insurance money from the barn fire and all of my parent's savings, they decided to build a new house just across the driveway next to where the barn once was. It wasn't going to be fancy, but we had to do something. The upholstery business was really taking off and it needed more room to grow. My parents hired our neighbor Levi who was a brick mason, to build the basement and then had a prefab house set on the basement blocks. The house came in two halves already built. Then the builders used a crane to attach the two halves together. It was pretty slick. It was very exciting watching all the work being done over a couple months.

A couple of the guys working on the roof asked my dad about the neighbor to the east. My dad told them that it would be Tim or that hermit guy that lives on Tim's land. The roofers said that they could see someone peeking from behind the trees on the other side of the fence line as they worked. One roofer even said, "It was hard to tell, but I think there were two guys." My dad shrugged it off and told me to wash out the wheelbarrow they had been using. I was always trying to help the crews clean up when I could. They even gave me a hammer of my own. Once the house was done, we moved all of our house furniture in. This wasn't as nice as the house my mom loved so much in Browndeer, but it was much nicer than the old rundown farmhouse. The new house came with a new fridge and my mom was so happy to see that there was even a dishwasher. The house came with electric heat, but my dad put a wood-burning stove in the basement to keep our electric bill from getting too high. Why not? We had all the wood we needed. There now were three small bedrooms. Mom and dad took the corner room, Wayne and Drew in the larger room, then Lonnie and Dean in the small room. That left me with sleeping in the living room. There was a couch that was a pull-out bed that I used. I really didn't mind. I considered it to be my room after everyone went to bed. The best thing about this house was there were two bathrooms. One for the boys and one for mom and dad. No more waiting for the bathroom! Well...at least less waiting.

It didn't take long for my dad to gradually move the business into the basement of the house. It was easy to just walk down one flight of stairs for everyone to get to work. Plus, we didn't have to heat the old farmhouse any longer. That saved us almost half the wood usage. We even were able to turn off the electricity in the old farmhouse. We now just used it for storage. My dad would see old furniture on the side of the street when he went into the cities and threw them into the back of the truck. We had Customers that were looking for furniture. They would select the piece they wanted and the materials they liked. It was a way to help make money for the business. We even had a judge from Portage that liked to stop by and pick out a couple pieces every year. He would bring his wife and they would stay for dinner and drinks. Just another opportunity for my dad to tell all his long-winded stories.

19

CAMPING

Age 6

I t was late August and since it was the last weekend before school started my older brothers decided they wanted to camp out up in our woods. They asked Dad during lunch, and he was totally fine with it. I said, "I want to camp too." Of course, they said no, but my dad told them then no one was going.

Drew replied, "You better not chicken out in the middle of the night!"

I said with great eagerness and a big smile on my face, "Of course, I won't!"

My dad said, "There's an old army tent and blankets you guys could use stored in the farmhouse."

Once we were done working for the day, we grabbed the tent, blankets, pillows, along with some drinks, pizza burgers, a loaf of bread and beans that we would cook on the fire. We loaded the truck with all our supplies and drove into the woods. About halfway through the woods, we found a nice clearing with a big oak tree in the center. We unloaded all our supplies and set up the tent, built a fire from the wood they cut and the sticks I picked up from around the campsite. My brothers also brought my dad's pistols. Just In case we run into a bear, wolves or mountain lion. They teased me by saying if a bear attacked, all they had to do was be able to run faster than me. That the bear would eat me, and they would get away. I didn't let them scare me. While I was picking up sticks, one of my brothers must have thought it would be funny to make calls like a bobcat crying in heat. It sounds a lot like a woman screaming but very growly. I told them, "Nice try!"

Drew replied, "Nice try what?"

"The bobcat screams!"

Then Wayne said, "I heard that too!" and kind of laughed. Drew said, "I heard something, but I was over in the other direction." I just chalked it up to them trying to scare me. Wayne eventually had a nice fire going and he cooked up the pizza burgers on an old cast iron frying pan my mom gave us. We ate them on just regular loaf bread. They were so good. Then we had marshmallows cooked on sticks that we had broken off a nearby tree. I preferred my marshmallows burnt. It was really fun hanging out in the woods at night. I just sat there listening to both of my brothers just joking around. They talked about a show they had recently watched. Monty Python Flying Circus! I laid on my back on a fallen tree that was nearby and watched the stars overhead. You could hear crickets chirping and see bats flying around in and above the canopy of trees. There were shooting stars zipping by and an owl hooting loudly that echoed through the woods in the background. It sounded more like a whoop. Wayne said, "I that owl is pissed that we are up here!" We heard it a few times, but it must have taken off. We all just sat around the fire talking and getting lost into the flames till about midnight and finally turned in. We all were dead tired. There was plenty of room in the tent for the three of us. Wayne and Drew tried to scare me just as they turned out the lantern. They whispered, "Did you hear that?" Drew said, "Ya, what was that?" I lay there listening. All I heard was a branch break. They said, "I think it's a bear!" They laughed and said, "We can throw Jacob out there and make our getaway!" I just ignored them, rolled over and went to sleep. When we woke and started packing up, Wayne noticed there was a tree branch that was laying over the hood of the truck. Wayne asked me, "Why would you leave a branch on the hood?" I said, "I didn't." Drew said, "I didn't!" Wayne just pulled it off, and we finished loading the truck. The branch had a fresh break, so I looked at the trees by the truck and there were no signs of branches missing. We were using dead branches for the fire the night before. We only broke off fresh branches to cook the marshmallows. Those branches were from the other side of the camp, away from the truck. We threw them into the fire after we were done using them last night. Then we could hear my dad whistling for us down at the farm. We finished cleaning the area up and headed home. I had a lot of fun and enjoyed our night of independence. But I definitely prefer my bed to sleeping on the ground. I was very sore and tired the whole day.

20

WHO'S THROWING ROCKS?

Age 7

We have now lived in our new house for about a year now. It was so much more comfortable and efficient than the old and run-down farmhouse. Everything was new. The business was doing so well that my dad added on a large two-story garage to use as an added workshop for the auto upholstery. The garage had a regular size garage door and then one that we could fit a large box truck into on the other end. To heat the garage, my dad added another wood-burning stove. So, we were right back to needing enough wood to fuel two stoves again. I was now using a chainsaw and able to drive the truck and tractor (not legally) to go up in the woods to cut wood. I was up there a lot by myself. I actually loved being up in the woods. There always was the hustle and bustle of activity of my parents, brothers, pets, the upholstery business and the farm animals. It was nice to have a little peace and quiet. The woods were that for me. I would, on occasion, see deer, owls, squirrels, quail, foxes, pheasants, foxes, hawks, turkeys, bobcats and so many birds. They didn't bother me, so I didn't bother them. Experiencing so much just made me feel so connected to nature. I would always mimic all the birds by chirping and whistling back. Click at the squirrels and so on. If I heard a noise, I copied it and most of the time, they would respond. Even though we didn't understand each other, I felt as though we were having conversations. One time I was loading some wood into the trailer near the back fence line and some squirrels were chattering, so I chattered back. They would chatter and I would chatter back.

Then as I was throwing a piece of wood into the trailer, a small rock hit the ground and rolled by me. I thought, *what the heck?* I thought the squirrels were dropping rocks at me. I looked up and couldn't see any squirrels, though.

I continued to load the wood when another rock went zipping through the leaves of a few trees and lands just past me. At this time, I knew it couldn't have been any squirrels. So, I picked up the rock and launched it back in the direction it came from and yelled, "Knock it off!" I thought it was possibly one or both of my older brothers. Maybe they were trying to scare me. It wouldn't be the first time. The both of them just loved to pick on me. I finished loading the trailer and I took a drink of water and yelled out, "If you want a ride back down, I'm leaving." I didn't see or hear anything. I started up the tractor and headed back to the farm. I pulled up and went into the shop and there were my two older brothers. I asked my mom if they had left the shop at all. She said, "They hadn't left the shop all day." So, I'm not sure who was throwing rocks at me. I didn't say anything about it to anyone and thought maybe it could have been our neighbor Brett's son, Gus. Gus, just like my brothers, liked to pick on me as well and maybe he had tried to be funny. I saw Gus a couple days later when he was driving by. He stopped to see my older brothers, so I asked him if he was throwing rocks at me in the woods. He said that they don't go that far back into their woods that butts up against our woods. He said that his dad Brett doesn't even hunt that far back. He said he's never really been back there. Only once with his dad to mend the fence line a few years ago.

So I'm not sure who was throwing rocks, but I knew there was nothing I could do about it for now. Maybe it was the stranger I had seen previously. I guess I'll have to just keep my eyes open.

21

TORNADO

Age 7

It's now a hot late dogs' day of a summer day in August. What made it worse was the humidity. The air was so thick and heavy. We didn't have air conditioning back then, so as kids, we would often use a garden hose to cool off. We had a water well drilled deep in the ground and a pump forced it up to the house. The water always stayed at a consistent cool 58°. Sometimes we would hook up the sprinkler and run under the water. It was cold enough to take your breath away. It really wasn't like we were playing in the water. We did it just to keep cool. Between the farm work and the upholstery business, we were working about 10-12 hours every day. My older brothers mainly stayed in the shop most of the day. I would help take the material off the furniture and car seats and they would put the new materials back on. Then I would be responsible for all the feeding and care for all the animals. I would take the horses out for a ride a few times a week. It was one of my favorite chores that I did. The horses all had different personalities, but they all loved to go for a ride. I would take them up into the upper field near the woods, but none of the horses ever wanted to go into the woods. They all would freak out if we even got too close. They can sense danger and it was possible that coyotes, a black bear, another wolf or a cougar could be lurking in the shadows.

I would also cut the grass a couple days a week. We had plenty of yard, so it would take a couple hours with my push mower. I spent a lot of my time in the woods cutting and splitting wood to burn over the winter. I usually tried to be up in the woods during the heat of the day because it was about 10° cooler up there. Most of my day was by myself and out of the shop. Even when I was working inside, I was out in the new garage, away from my mom and dad. I actually loved being alone. Even though my dad gave me a list of things to do every day, I was kind of my own boss. It was up to me to get the work done on that list each day. When I would report back to my dad with all my duties done, I always felt a sense of pride as I rattled them off.

On this day, after we ate dinner, I took the horses for a ride and afterward, I put them in the pasture across the street with the cows to graze. The horses had a small horse shelter they could go into and the hickory trees to hang out under with lots of grass. They really loved to be there where they could run free on several acres of open space. After dinner, we all sat and watched a TV show and went to bed as usual around ten pm. There was a large window fan in the living room that drew air out from the house. I enjoyed it since it was right next to where I slept in the living room. I enjoyed the comforting breeze as I slept. It was right about midnight when I was awakened by a really strong wind blowing. It was loud and rattling the windows. It was even slowing down the window fan. The wind was blowing even harder as I jumped up and the window fan was now blowing backward, and sparks were now flying across the house. The noise outside sounded like nothing I'd heard before. It sounded like a freight train running through the house. The whole house was shaking, and I could hear my whole family behind me as I made my way away from the front windows that sounded like they were about to break toward the hallway. My dad yelled, "Get into the basement quickly!" We started to make our way to the basement. As we walked by the living room, the fan blew out of the window and went crashing into the wall. We all ran downstairs and hid under my mom's large woodwork table. By the time we all got under the table, the shaking stopped and there was silence. The power was out, but my dad had grabbed a flashlight and we hurried back upstairs. We slowly opened the door to look outside. My dad told us kids to stay inside. You could hear a roaring off in the distance up towards the woods. My dad flashed the light around and started saying, "Oh my God!" Over and over! He was in shock. I peered out the front door to see what he was looking at. Our water pump house was gone. The old farmhouse garage was gone. The tractor shop was gone. The granary was gone. The back horse sheds were gone. Then we saw that the old farmhouse was still there along with the new garage and the workshop was still there. We walked across the road and the horses and cows were all ok and were at the bottom of the field. The pigs and chicken were good. The corn crib was good as well. We were lucky we were still alive. There had been no warning. We didn't have a thunderstorm or rain. Nothing!

Then the power came back on. We all went back to bed and felt a little lucky.

As we woke in the morning, it was like waking up to a war zone. Half the farm was gone. I mean, it literally was gone. The only thing left was the old foundations of all those buildings. The rest of the buildings weren't found anywhere around. There wasn't much debris to even pick up. The tornado had gone right up our driveway and up the side of the hill and then into the woods, where it looked as though God had parted the trees just like you would part someone's hair. A straight line of trees ripped out of the ground and fallen trees on both sides. We were lucky that the horses were across the street in the open field. They were all ok. They would have been killed if they were in the horse sheds. The sheds were completely gone.

A couple days later, we had some neighbors about two miles away that heard about the tornado say they found tin roofing and lots of old wood boards on their property. I made my way to the woods to inspect the damage. When I got to the top of the hill, I could now see how powerful the tornado was. There must have been close to fifty trees down. Some were over three feet across. This was now my mission is to clean this mess up.

22

PICKING CORN/TURKEYS

Age 7

I t was now a sunny but cool, crisp October day. I liked it when fall came around with all the colors of the leaves and we were no longer having trouble sleeping due to the hot temps and humidity. Those nights are just so uncomfortable. The cornfield was now ready to be picked, but we had one rather large problem. The tractor broke down and we didn't have enough money to fix it. The tractor was almost thirty years old, and the engine and gearbox needed a lot of work. But my dad having me around, figured that I could pick it by hand with the wheelbarrow versus asking a neighbor to help pick it for us. I was free labor. I got started and was making good progress over the first week or so. I would chop the corn off with a machete, fill the wheelbarrow, haul it to the corn crib and shovel it out. I would work till it started getting dark out. The deer would always venture and hang out by the edge of the woods just before dusk and wait till I left the field and then start eating the corn.

After the second week, I was about halfway done. Then on the third week, it started snowing. I had to trudge through the snow, plus I was pushing a wheelbarrow full of corn. I had to reduce my loads of corn to only half full now. There was no way I was able to push a full load with all the snow. It was taking much longer to get each load back to the corn crib. After the fifth week, I had finally picked the whole fifteen acres of corn. I was so proud. I ran in and told my dad I had it all done! He said, "Good! Now start cutting down all the corn stalks and bring them up so the horses, cows and pigs can use them for bedding." I stood there for a second. I thought I was done in the field. So, I grabbed my hat, coat and gloves and headed right back out and started cutting all the stalks down and hauling them back to the farm. I was lucky. The stalks were all dry and lightweight. I could stack a lot in the wheelbarrow.

I was about three-quarters of the way done and one morning, the DNR dropped off four turkeys at the bottom of the cornfield. They wandered around for about an hour or so, looking for food. I picked all the corn already, so they weren't finding much. On my next trip, I grabbed some of the shelled corn and threw it their way. They gobbled it up. I was working my way back to the farm and kept throwing them corn. So, they followed me. I then thought I wondered if they wanted to stay at the farm. They would gobble and cluck, so I did the same. They would reply. So, I kept feeding them and gobbling all the way to the chicken pen. I fed them a good amount and they seemed content. I put some cornstalks in the pen, and they started to relax. I had put a top over the chicken pen and reinforced it around the bottom so that predators couldn't get in. I went inside and told my dad we now had four turkeys. My mom overheard me and said in disbelief, "What?"

I said, "I had four turkeys follow me and I have them in the chicken pen."

My dad said, "I have to see this!" So, we walked out, and he said, "I'll be damned." My dad patted me on the head and said, "I guess you're good for something." They seemed to like it in the chicken pen. After a week, I left the door open to let them out and they didn't want to come out. I was feeding all the animals nearby, so eventually, they made their way out and started following me around. I threw some feed and corn into their pen, and they ran back in. I think they liked their new life. I headed back to the field and was getting closer to the upper field when I heard some branches break. I had our dog Smokey hanging out with me. It was ok to have him in the field but not in the woods. We didn't want them chasing any deer away. Smokey looked intensely toward the woods, where I heard the branches break. He stood there motionless for a minute. Then we heard another branch break. Smokey started to growl. I thought it could be a deer or maybe a bear. So, I yelled out, "Hey Bear! Stay away, Bear!" Just like my dad told me to. Smokey finally stopped growling and we heard no more noises from the woods. Smokey would lay between me and the fence line. I think he wanted to be in between me and any possible danger. I petted him and thanked him for being so brave. I kept on working on those cornstalks. By the time I finished cutting all the corn stalks down, it was almost Christmas.

23

PAIN

Age 8

I was now eight years old, and I was working a lot more in the shop. My dad was starting to yell and get more upset than normal. He would get angry at us boys for the smallest things. He was also drinking a lot more. Every evening he would have a few drinks or more after dinner till bedtime and then go pass out in bed. My dad always liked to golf and would always take one of us boys with him to pull his clubs around the course. Recently he started renting a golf cart and he would let us drive the cart. That was a lot more fun for us, but we all have been noticing that he really had a hard time standing up straight as he got out of the golf cart. After one golf outing where he was President of the golf league, he seemed like he was in a lot of pain and was drinking heavily. After leaving the clubhouse, we stopped at another two taverns where he had a few drinks at each. We had been gone almost all day and it was just before the sun was setting. My dad was driving us home and he was swerving badly. I was getting a little worried about our safety. We were about halfway home, and all of a sudden, there were flashing blue and red lights in the mirrors. My dad said, "Don't say a word. I'll do the talking."

A tall, well-groomed officer walked up to my dad and said, "I noticed you were swerving a lot back there."

My dad replied, "Sorry, I was swatting at mosquitoes."

The officer chuckled and said, "I do smell alcohol."

"I had a couple after golfing." My dad admitted. The officer looked at me and asked, "Are you able to drive?" I was tall for my age and had driven tractors and trucks on the farm all the time. So, my answer was "Yes." He said to my dad, "I suggest that he drives the rest of the way home, or I'll be forced to take you in for DWI." My dad gave the officer a nod and said, "No problem, Sir." The officer didn't ask me if I had a driver's license. We switched seats and I was now really nervous. I had never driven on the road before. Of course, my dad was now already giving me driving lessons. I took off slowly and got up to 50mph. I had never driven this fast. The most was maybe 20mph on the dirt paths around the farm. I didn't even know the laws of driving. I just did what my parents had done when they drove. We were about home and my dad had passed out. I was fine with that since he was stressing me out anyway. I pulled up into the driveway and my mom was looking out the window since she expected us to be home much earlier. She had my two older brothers come out and help put Dad to bed. Once we got him in bed, my mom was clearly upset. I then said to my mom, "I noticed he was having a hard time standing up and he has been getting angry very easily lately. He has been yelling at us boys more often."

My mom replied, "He has increasingly been in more pain. His back mostly but his knees, neck, hands and feet." She added, "I've been telling him that he needs to go see the doctor, but I can't get him to go." My dad had a distrust for the military doctors throughout his twenty-two years in the service. My mom said, "His pain started out slowly with just aches and pains, so he would take Excedrin. It would help some, but now years later, it was not helping." My dad had a hard life growing up before the military on a cotton farm in central Alabama. They had to use mules to pull a plow and they picked all the corn and cotton crops by hand. He also played sports like most kids growing up. He also played quarterback for a semi-pro team, the Alameda Wild Cats, while stationed in Alameda, California.

Now that he was in his forty's, the pain started really creeping in. To combat the pain, he now is self-medicating by drinking himself to sleep every night. It was very sad. His heavy drinking kept on for another ten years. His short temper continued as well.

24

THE SCREAMING LADY

Age 8

My neighbor, and friend, Thad, was hanging out with me on a warm Sunday afternoon. Normally he never came over because my dad would think that any of our friends would want to help, and he would put them to work as well. So, it was rare anyone would want to stop by. Thad and I were throwing rocks and clumps of dirt from around the cornfield. We didn't care what we were throwing at, but we would make a game out of it. He would yell out, "I bet I can hit that fence post first!" Then we would start launching rocks at it until one of us would hit it! Then I would yell out, "I bet I can hit that tree first! We would do this for hours. Playing this game would also help me with my control when I was pitching or throwing a baseball.

We were halfway down the cornfield when we heard this scream come from the woods. It sounded like a lady screaming in distress. We've heard our neighbor's sister scream before, but this sounded more like an older person in serious trouble! We also had a neighbor a few miles away that had goats and this wasn't goats. I've heard bobcat mating screams and mountain lion screams as well. This was not any animal. It sounded like a woman. The weird thing was that they weren't yelling for help. Just a blood-curdling scream that echoed through the woods. Thad and I walked over to the edge of the woods, but it stopped. We both yelled, "Do you need help?" We heard nothing. We ran down to the farm, where we told my mom. My dad was away picking up furniture and, most likely, hitting a few bars on the way home.

My mom asked, "Are you sure it sounded like a woman?" We both said, "Yes!"

My mom said, "Maybe we should take the truck up there and see if anyone was up there lost or something." So, we jumped in the truck and headed up the hill. We drove slowly through the woods, stopping and shutting off the truck and yelling, "Hello! Anyone out there?" We stopped about four times with no reply. My mom said, "It must have been a kid screaming like kids do." Thad and I just looked at each other and thought that that didn't make sense. We tried our best to see if anyone needed help.

It felt weird leaving the woods. My mom and I dropped off Thad at his house. On the way home, I asked if we could go look again. She said no that she had to make dinner. While she was making dinner, I sat on top of the truck down by the farm for a couple hours as it became dark with a flashlight shining toward the woods. I saw a few deer along the top of the cornfield, but there were no more screams. Whatever it was, it made me think that someone was in distress, and I had a hard time going to sleep thinking we couldn't help her. The next morning, I took the tractor up and drove the complete path all the way around the woods. I would stop and listen, but there was no more yelling or any signs of a person. I thought to myself that someday I sure hope to not find this person's bones up there.

25

WHAT WAS THAT?

Age 9

It was now early summer, and I had just finished the 4th grade. I really enjoyed being in school and loved to learn new things. Working on the farm was great, but every year it was really becoming more like work than fun. Our dad was increasingly showing his anger toward us boys. It didn't take much to set him off. It was to the point that I didn't want to be near him. Being outside, away from him or in the woods, was the best place for me. I just didn't want to hear him always yelling at everyone. I think he could sense that I didn't like the situation and maybe was making him a little more resentful and more upset with me.

This day I was getting ready to head up to the woods to cut up trees and my two older brothers and my younger brother Lonnie were standing outside the back door when we heard this thunderous sound come from the eastern corner of the woods about one hundred yards away. It was like a loudspeaker with a lot of bases and someone angrily said, "Raaa!" You could feel it!

I said, "What was that?"

Wayne right away said, "I don't know, but it sounds really big and pissed off!" Lonnie looked really scared, just took off and ran into the house. Wayne and Drew grabbed a gun and wanted to go see what it was. I was watching the woods and thinking, *I don't think it's such a good idea to go up there today. Whatever that was really sounded big and angry.* It didn't sound like anything I'd ever heard before. I've even heard a bear roar, and this was twenty times as powerful. I was actually scared. I could hear my dad yelling at my older brothers to put the guns back and get into the shop and get to work. I waited for my dad to go downstairs to the shop. I snuck into the house and went into the gun closet and grabbed his Colt 45 and grabbed the 30/30 rifle. I made sure they were loaded and had extra rounds for both. I put them into the truck and headed for the lower end of the field on the edge, away from where we heard the noise to cut wood. I wasn't going anywhere near where that noise came from. I didn't see anything or hear anything, but I always kept the 45 holstered on me and the rifle in the truck. I still couldn't figure out what that was. When we all gathered for lunch, Wayne brought it up in conversation. My dad said it was probably one of the neighbors or a cow or something. Drew then said, "I've never heard anything like that." Wayne said, "Ya, it was so loud I could feel it." I said, "I felt it too. Like it was standing right next to me." My dad shook his head and pretty much thought we were exaggerating what we heard and that was the last we spoke of it. I just knew that the woods could be very dangerous and that I would always be alert and keep the guns with me. I absolutely wanted no part of whatever that was.

26

STRANGER IS BACK!

Age 10

Another year had gone by and it's now my favorite time of the year, summer. I have been extremely busy helping Wayne take apart the auto upholstery and learning to put it back together. I was also now finally getting paid. It wasn't much, but as my dad would remind us often that we had food on the table and a roof over our heads. We would work after school till about 9 or 10 PM, 7 AM till 7 PM on Saturday's and 7 AM till noon on Sundays. I would save my $5 a week and sometimes we would walk to the General Store in town about a three-mile walk each way to go get a soda or candy bar. We didn't have sweets in the house very often and if we did, it didn't last long with five boys. During the summer, we worked from 7 AM till 7 PM except for Sunday from 7 AM till noon. And yes, I still made only $5 a week.

Besides the shop work, I still took care of the animals. We now had ducks, geese and rabbits added to our assortment of animals. Then I, of course, was cutting wood for the winter again. I had most of the fallen trees cleaned up and I learned in school that if I cut the lower branches off the trees, they would grow taller. I started trimming the lower branches off the rows of pine trees at the edge of the woods. The branches went all the way to the ground, and they were so thick you couldn't see from row to row. As I was about halfway done, I heard some heavy footsteps at the end of the row. I thought Drew or Wayne were running around trying to scare me. I just yelled out, "You guys don't scare me." I didn't hear any reply. Then a saw out of the corner of my eye something run by where I had started cutting the branches off. It was dark and hairy. I quickly grabbed the 45 pistols I had holstered. I yelled a warning.

"I have a gun and I'll use it!" I yelled, "If this is Wayne or Drew you guys better knock it off. It's not funny." I heard nothing. I thought maybe it was the really tall guy I had seen several years before. So, I yelled out, "This is our property and you're not welcome!" I also yelled again, "I have a gun!" Still nothing. It kind of freaked me out a little and I felt unsafe, so I packed up and went back to the house. Wayne was in the garage working and Drew was in the shop. I just casually asked my mom if they had left the house at all. She said, "No, they had been here the whole time."

So not sure what the heck I saw. The next day my dad sent me back up to finish the pine rows. I was over yesterday, and I had the guns with me. As I was working my way, I then looked down and could see a large barefoot foot track in the sand. I put my foot next to it and it was almost twice the size, and I was wearing boots. I thought it must have been that guy again. I scanned the woods and saw no trace of anyone. I finished cutting the pine branches off and loaded them all into the trailer. The pine sap in the branches and needles were great for starting fires. I told my dad that I thought that the tall guy was back around because I had found a footprint again. He said, "Well, let's go take a look." We got into the truck and drove up there. We walked around and I showed him the print. My dad said, "Damn, this guy's got huge feet." We looked to see if there were any other prints. But we couldn't find anything. Then we drove around the woods, looking around for any clues of maybe someone hunting on our land. We found nothing. My dad even complemented me on how nice the woods looked. I felt pretty good about that. It was rare he ever gave me a compliment. We got back to the farm, and he said just be careful up there and keep a gun on you. I said I already did. I pulled out his 45 and the 30-30 rifle. He said, "Good! If any issues shoot first, ask questions later." I was a good shot and always have felt very comfortable shooting them.

27

ALABAMA

Age 11

I was now 11 years old, and we were headed to Alabama to visit my dad's side of the family for Easter school break. We all loaded up for the drive at 4 am. We had a box truck that had bunk beds on both sides and a bed with storage under it in the back. I loved going on trips. It was so exciting. Whenever we would go there, our neighbor Brett and his son Gus would be kind enough to take care of our animals. Not having to work the farm and shop for two weeks was a welcome blessing. It was also great to go south to warmer weather after having such long winters. It was always a long drive of about two days each way. I loved just watching all the scenery out the window. You could actually smell the warmth the further south we got. I really enjoyed these trips. We didn't have to work, and it was always an adventure for me to drive across the country. There was so much to see on such long drives. We were driving on the freeway in Tennessee when my dad yelled to us, "Check it out. It's the Judd's tour bus." As we drove by, I waved, and they waved back! I knew who they were since my dad always listened to country music and I've seen them on the TV show *Hee Haw*. I thought that was pretty cool.

On the second day of driving, we finally arrived at my Granny's house, where my dad grew up. My dad's dad had passed before I was born, so I never knew him. My dad's sister, Aunt Sissy, lived there with her husband, Uncle Thomas. They had a daughter, Shelby and her husband, Lee. They had 2 kids, Skeeter, who was my age and Tucker, who was two years younger. Skeeter and I would hang out together whenever we came down. We would walk to the convenience store to get soda and candy. We also liked to play catch and play games. My Granny was a stern person with no sense of humor. She didn't say much, but when she did, you had better listen or she would pinch your butt and it hurt. I could see where my dad got his sternness from. My dad would take us around and show us the area where he grew up, went to school and then, of course, all our relatives that lived nearby. It was great to visit them since they would always have good food that they would prepare for us. I really enjoyed southern cooking except for grits and chitlins. Chitlins are cooked pig intestines. Yuk!

My dad's relatives would tell stories and I could see my dad felt like he was home again and in his element. I wished he could always be like that. He just never sat down with any of us and had real conversations. It was always as if he was our boss, or we were in the military, and he was the ranking officer. We always were required to say, "Yes Sir, No Sir." If we didn't, he would yell, "What did you say to me?" I guess so many years in the military made him the way he is. Nearly every time we would come down here, my dad's younger brother Edward that was a Colonel in the Army would show up, and all hell would break loose. My dad being enlisted and my uncle being an officer, they would like to poke insults at each other in a weird loving way. I thought it was pretty funny, but you could tell they loved each other but would never say it or admit it. It always seemed such a simple life when we visited. I always enjoyed our visits and, most of all, the way they would talk with their Southern drawl! They had a definite accent. My Aunt Sissy would say things that were only said by Southerners like to turn on the fan, she would say, "Mash that button!" I found them all very entertaining. By the time we would leave, I was almost speaking the same accent as they do. But after two weeks away, I couldn't wait to get back to the farm. It was hard work, but it was home.

28

THE LAKE

Age 12

Summer has arrived once again, with lots of sunshine and warm winds from the southwest pouring over the farm. I was now 12 years old. My dad and I went on an estimate call for some boat seats to recover. It was at lake Jordan about four miles away from the farm. This lake was surrounded by really nice houses, and nearly all the houses had boats and jet skis tied up at their docks. These people had money! The owner took us down to his dock and showed us his boat. My dad inspected the seats and talked to the guy about how much it was going to cost. The guy agreed, and we started taking the seats out. The guy sent out his son Clay who was the same age as me. He helped me carry them up to the van and load them. It was nice having help. It was quite the hill to go up to get back to the car. Clay asked a lot of questions about what I did and what and where we lived. I explained we had the farm and the upholstery shop just a few miles away. He thought that was pretty cool. I found out that they were from the suburbs of Chicago, and this was their summerhouse. I always thought that it would be awesome to have a cabin on a lake. We took the seats home and recovered them in a few days. My dad and I took them back and Clay again helped me, this time installing them back into the boat. My dad was enjoying a beer with Clay's dad while we worked.

When we were done, Clay asked if he and I could go for a ride in the boat. Both of our dads said, "Sure!" They were happy just hanging out there and drinking. Clay took us around the lake. I had never ridden in a boat before. It was so cool! The smell of the lake, the wind blowing in my face were great. Then he stopped at the dock at the end of the lake where there was a resort and bar that my dad has stopped by with me before on one of his many business trips to give estimates or pick up furniture. Clay filled the gas tank up and we went inside to pay. Inside there was a small game room with video games like Asteroids, PAC Man, Phoenix and a pinball machine. Clay asked, "Do you want to play some? "I said, "I have no cash on me." Clay said, "No problem. My dad gave me $25." Clay ordered a couple cheeseburgers, fries and some quarters to play games with. He gave me a dollars' worth and said, "Have fun." I really have never played video games before. So, I watched Clay play first, then I would play. It was fun, but I wasn't that good at it at first. We ate the cheeseburgers and fries. We talked like we were friends forever. He seemed interested in my life and was looking for someone to hang out with. The conversation just flowed naturally. Then he ordered a pizza for his dad to take back. Once we got back, my dad was ready to go. Clay said, "Here's our number." So I gave him ours. He said, "If you want to go boating Sunday afternoon, call me."

All week I looked forward to hopefully getting to go over to the lake. I made sure that I did all my work and chores. Then Sunday at lunch, I asked my dad if I could go over there for the afternoon. I said, "I have all my chores done." He was reluctant, but I threw in there that maybe I would be able to get some more boat owners to get their boats reupholstered. He handed me a dozen business cards to hand out and said, "Be careful on your bike and be back by dark." I jumped on my bike and met Clay at the resort area. He was inside the arcade, and he welcomed me with a yell! "Dude! You made it!" I said, "Oh ya! I've been looking forward to it." He then called over a couple friends,

Tom and Jeff. He introduced them to me, and we shook hands. They seemed like nice guys. They were both from the Chicago area. As we were leaving the resort, two beautiful girls were walking our way when Clay yelled out, "You guys are late!" They said, "No, we're not!" Then Clay introduced me to Carrie and Kelsey. They were from the Milwaukee area. All I knew was these girls were the prettiest girls I'd ever seen. They had makeup on, earrings, bracelets and white boating clothes. I had never seen girls so dressed up. I was just wearing a white T-shirt and blue Jean shorts that I had cut off and my only pair of old tennis shoes. I kind of fit in with the guys. We then all loaded into the boat. The guys were in the back and the girls in the front. As we took off, all I could smell was their perfume. I had never smelled perfume on any girls before, only on my mom and older women. Clay drove us to the other end of the lake and had me throw out the anchor. Clay said, "This looks like a good spot to go swimming." The guys all took off their shirts and we jumped in. The girls sat there for a minute. The water was great! It was so refreshing. Then the girls took off their shorts and shirts, revealing their two-piece bathing suits. Again, I had never seen girls in bathing suits before. They both jumped in while plugging their noses. We all swam around for about half an hour before Clay said, "What ya say, we head back and get something to eat." The guys loaded back in the boat and then the girls needed help getting in, so I reached out my hand. Kelsey grabbed my hand and I think I blacked out! A girl was holding my hand. Then I helped her sister Carrie in.

Again...I blacked out for a few seconds. We headed back when Carrie sat next to me and asked a few questions about me. I was not sure what I told her because, again, I was in shock that she was talking to me. Once we got back to the resort, we ordered food and I bought Clay's burger to repay him. They all were asking questions about who I was, what I did and where we lived. Kelsey then says, "Oh, you're a 'local'." I wasn't sure how to feel about that. They all were all on summer vacation and their families would come up to the resort most weekends. It was getting late. I didn't want to leave, but I had to get back before dark. They all said they would be back next weekend and asked if I could hang out with them. I got on my bike and started my four-mile ride home. It felt really good to be accepted into their group of friends. As I was riding back home, I was riding on the back side of our country block when I heard something in the woods about twenty-five yards in. I slowed down to see if it was a deer. I couldn't see anything, so I continued. Then I could hear branches break again but directly in the woods alongside me. Whatever it was following me, it seemed. It kind of freaked me out, so I then rode faster. The noise continued for about another half mile. It was starting to scare me. Every now and then, I could hear a branch crack or whatever it was pushing through the tree's branches. The noises stopped as I went by Tim's farm. Whatever it was didn't seem to be following me any longer. After that, I really didn't think about it and got back to thinking about the lake. I was just so excited for the next weekend! I had made new friends; they treated me like a person, unlike my brothers. This was a totally different world than what I was used to on the farm. I wanted to go over as often as I could. We all became friends and they would call me when they were coming to town. Lots of boating, swimming, fishing and just hanging out. They were very different than all my farmer friends!

29

THE CABIN

Age 13

Our big family was about to lose one when my oldest brother Wayne was going into the Marines. I wasn't sure how it was going to be without him around. Even though he liked to pick on me a lot, he was my big brother. Somebody I could rely on to help and protect me when needed. I knew I would miss his goofy sense of humor. My parents threw him a going-away party. They invited neighbors, family and friends to the farm to see him off and wish him good luck. It was the first time we ever had a party at the farm. Then he was off to boot camp in San Diego. It was hard without him home. He had always been there my whole life. It took some getting used to. After a few months, he called home and said he was going to graduate. My dad decided to fly out by himself for the graduation ceremony. While he was gone, I decided to slack a little and start building a small cabin up on the edge of the woods that you could see over the farm. I always wanted to build a fort growing up but never had the time. We were always busy working the farm and upholstery business. So, I started by cutting trees into logs and cut out notches like a Lincoln log cabin. The logs were all about twelve feet long and ten to twelve inches in diameter. Each log weighed about two hundred fifty pounds or more. So, I used the tractor bucket to stack the logs as I cut them. Then I made a center beam across the top and then the roof. I cut out a doorway and put in an old door from the corn crib that was laying around. I brought in some flat stones from along the edge of the field to build a fireplace. I stacked them nice and neat. I even built a bench on the front that you could sit on and watch over the whole farm. I was having the time of my life. It took several days for me to get it built. It wasn't perfect, but it was mine. I then had to hurry to get all my normal work done on the farm before my dad would get back from San Diego. When I got down to the house, there was bad news on the phone. My mom said that she had heard from the hospital in San Diego. She had this worried look in her eyes. She said that dad was mugged after being in a bar. They said he was going to be ok but couldn't fly for a week due to a bad concussion. They caught the guy that night, and he was arrested. My dad rested for a few days and then caught a military flight back home. He had to have nine stitches in his head where the guy hit him with the butt of his gun.

It was good to see he was ok, but he definitely looked a little rough. The day after he got back, he sent me up to cut wood. As I drove by my new cabin, I couldn't believe my eyes. The cabin was torn all to pieces. The logs were spread all over the place. It was completely leveled. The first thing I did was turn back around and head straight for my brother Drew. I started yelling at him, "Why would you do that? I worked so hard on that!"

He looked at me dumbfounded and said, "What are you talking about?"

I said, "The cabin?"

"What cabin?"

"The one I just built!"

He still acted like I was crazy and that he had nothing to do with it. I was livid! My mom then said, "What on earth are you yelling about?" I told her I had been building a cabin and that Drew had to of torn it apart. She didn't know about the cabin and said, "You weren't supposed to be building a cabin anyway." Then Drew stepped in and said, "I didn't know that you had built a cabin!"

"Then who torn it to pieces?"

"I don't know, but I didn't do it." I just left and went back up there. Drew followed me and saw what I was talking about. He said, "Holy crap, you did build a cabin." Then said as he laughed, "You must have not built it very well!" I then thought that he would have had to use the tractor to do this, but the cabin wasn't just pushed over. The logs were littered everywhere. Some of the logs were on top of small trees that were standing before. I was perplexed and pissed off. I even yelled at an owl to stop hooting that seemed to be laughing behind me at a distance. So out of complete frustration, I just grabbed the chainsaw and cut all the logs into firewood and took them down to the farm. I wasn't about to waste my time trying to put it back together again. All I knew was that whoever tore it down was messing with me and that I would figure it out someday.

30

CHANGES

Age 13

My everyday life was about to change. With my oldest brother Wayne, who was now stationed in Guantánamo Bay, Cuba, I was needed more in the shop. I had taken over all the auto upholstery and was helping take apart almost all the furniture. Drew now is enlisted in the Navy and is going to Great Lakes Naval Academy in the spring. On top of my two older brothers' changes, I came home one day from school with very saddening news. My dad had sold the horses to the Ringling Brothers Circus in Baraboo. I couldn't believe it. He didn't even mention the possibility of selling them to any of us. I loved the horses and I thought we would have them forever. He also wanted to whittle down the animals on the farm so that we all could focus more on the business.

My dad then said, "Give me a head count on all the animals." So, I went around the farm and counted eight pigs, four turkeys, three ducks, five chickens and 0 horses. He knew I was not happy with the horses gone. He said, "The horses are going to be well cared for and it was too expensive to have them around." He added, "You're the only person that ever rode them." It was just a sad day for me. It did, however, lighten up my chores right away. The horses being gone did allow me to be in the shop more. Of course, I still needed to cut wood as long as I was able to get into the woods. So, since I was bummed out about the horses, I went to my safe place...the woods. It was always my place to just be alone. I had no one looking over my shoulder telling me what to do. I had the truck and trailer and pulled to the back of the woods. There was a hollow behind me that had some trees down up on the other side, but no way I could get to it. So, I cut up the trees that were on my side and started loading. It was getting to be late, and the sun was about to set. I grabbed a quick drink when I noticed what looked like someone's torso behind one of the fallen trees. I looked at it and it didn't move at all. It seemed to be much larger than what would be normal, so I thought that maybe it was a stump, and the shadows were playing tricks on my eyes. I didn't notice it when I had arrived. I kept looking at it, but nothing. I had to hurry to finish loading the wood. As I was getting into the truck, I looked again and now I couldn't see anything there. I thought that was weird. So, as I pulled the truck around and shined the headlights toward it and again saw nothing that looked like a torso. It was a little unnerving. I shrugged it off and took the load down to the farm and piled it up along the old barn wall. A few days later, I went back up to cut more wood. I drove by and stopped and looked at the downed trees across from the hollow and saw nothing that looked like a torso. So, I took a walk over there to check it out. As I looked around, you could see where the grass was matted down right where I had seen the torso. It was another situation where I shook my head and chalked it up to shadows and maybe it was just my imagination. I emptied the truck and trailer, stacking the wood along the old barn rock wall. My mom yelled out for me that dinner was ready. By the time I got to the table, everyone else was finished eating. My dad had his drinks already and had headed to bed. That was fine with me. My mom has fixed me a plate and sat with me at the table while I ate. I mentioned to her that I thought that someone was watching me in the woods across the hollow. Most likely that big guy I've seen in the past and his footprints around the farm. She said, "Are you sure you're not going crazy?"

I said, "I must be, but it sure gives me the creeps! Who would live as a hermit all by himself in the woods? With no shoes? Especially during the winter!" My mom replied, shaking her head, "I don't know, but always be careful up there." I finished my dinner and headed to bed.

31

MISSING

Age 14

It was once again my favorite time of the year...Summer! After a long winter cooped up in the house and shop, it was nice to finally get outside again. The first thing we did was have a nice sendoff party for Drew's departure for Navy Boot Camp yesterday. All his friends showed up, along with our neighbors and family members. It was great to have so many people show up. It was a Potluck party, so many brought a dish or desserts to pass around. So many tasted so good. It was nice getting to try something we normally wouldn't eat. Early the next morning, Dad took Drew to the bus station in Portage and sent him off to Great Lakes Naval Academy.

At fourteen years old, it was really on me to be a great help with the business with both of my older brothers gone now. My mom said to me after we ate breakfast, "You are now the man of the house." I replied with pride, "No problem, Mom. I will make sure that we keep building the business and helping out however I can." I hopped up and went straight to work.

I had just graduated eighth grade and was excited to be in high school next year. I was working the farm and feeding all the animals we had left when I noticed we were short a pig. I thought my dad had sold one and failed to tell me again. He would sell them to other farmers in the area for meat. So, I walked into the shop and asked him, "Did you get rid of one of the pigs?"

He said, "No, why?"

"Because we're short one."

He said, "Maybe you should go check the fence line. Maybe it dug under and got out." He then told me, "Hurry before any more find their way out." So, I walked inside and outside around the whole fence line. There was no evidence of anywhere it could possibly have gotten out at. I was perplexed. There was an area on the side facing the woods that looked like someone had been walking through the tall grass. It led back to the woods. I followed it but then lost the trail once I got into the woods. Then I could smell what smelled like roadkill that had been laying out in the sun. It was horrible. I looked around and thought, however, it had gotten out that a predator had killed it and left the rest to rot. I reluctantly followed the scent deeper into the woods. I couldn't find any dead animal carcass anywhere. I heard some twigs snapping off in the distance but couldn't see anything. I didn't have a gun on me at the time and thought it would be smart to head back right away. I reported back to my dad, and he said, "There's got to be a hole somewhere." So, we both walked the whole fence line again, checking it out and nothing. I showed him where the grass was laid down, so he and I followed it all the way into the woods together. We searched the area for about thirty minutes. At the very back of the woods, in a small hollow, we came across a large ledge of sandstone with some pine boughs that were laid in there for some bedding. There was no trace of a campfire or any belongings. As we got close, it really stunk under the ledge. My dad thought it might be this guy that I had seen and come across his footprints before. So, my dad pulled out all the pine boughs and he took out his gun and shot it in the air. He yelled out, "If you're around, this is a warning to stay off our property." Then he took the bullet casing out of the gun and put it on the ledge for him to see. All I knew was that I was a little creeped out that someone may be hanging out in our woods. Was he living up there or visiting occasionally, or what? I felt that if someone was living up there, they would need more shelter than a rock overhang and some pine boughs. It was all so confusing. I again made sure I didn't go into the woods without a gun on me and kept my head on a swivel.

32

ROCK CLAPPING

Age 14

It was a Sunday and summer was coming to a close, so after dinner, I decided to go run the hill behind the farm to get into shape for 8th. Grade football. Of course, I was always in pretty good shape, but football demanded you to be in better shape for all the running, hitting and tackling involved. So, I would sprint to the top and run back down as many times as I possibly could. I ran the hill and back five times before taking a breather and grabbing a drink of water. I felt like I could do a few more after taking a break. So, I continued to run up and then back down again. Each time I would count how long it took me to get to the top of the hill. Always pushing myself to beat my last time. It took forty-three seconds the first time. The second time it was forty-one seconds, and the third time, it was thirty-nine seconds. Then I took another break, grabbing some more water, and I also put on my football cleats to see how much they might help with traction. I tied them tight and dug in at my starting line. I took a deep breath and then I shot up the hill as fast as possible. I could tell right away that I would break my best time due to the traction I was getting with my cleats on. There was no slipping like my regular sneakers that I was wearing before. I flew past the finish line at the top of the hill. I was going so fast I had glided a short distance into the woods. The cool shade felt good since I had worked up such a sweat from all my running. I was cheering aloud to myself and chanting, "I beat my time! I beat my time! Yaaaa!" I ran the hill in thirty-three seconds! The football spikes had really helped.

I stood at the top of the hill overlooking the whole farm below and you could see for miles around. The sun was about to set, and the view was just amazing! There was an orangish/golden glow over the entire area. I wished I had our Polaroid camera to take a picture. I was just enjoying the beauty and cool breeze when suddenly, I was startled when I heard behind me in the woods what sounded like a clatter of rocks being hit together. There were about seven quick claps. I whipped around to see who was doing it. It was pretty loud, so they had to be close. I couldn't see anyone. Then it happened again. About six or seven really quick claps. It was really loud and echoed through the woods. I got the chills and started backing out of the woods while still watching for any movement. I saw nothing. Then I turned and started walking away when I heard a tree branch snap and turned to see something dark move across the area that I heard the noises from. It was too dark to see any details, but at that time, I just ran as fast as I could down the hill toward the farm. I slowed down and walked as I got close to the house. By that time, I thought that it must have been that guy again. He obviously didn't want to hurt me but seemed as if he was protecting his territory like an animal would. I went inside after watching the woods for a while, not seeing anything. My mom said I needed to take a shower and get ready for bed. My dad still wasn't home from his business trip. Obviously, stopping at a few bars on his way home. So, I told her that I think there still is this guy living up in the woods like a hermit. He most likely lives in Tim, our neighbors' woods. I told her about the rock clapping, and she looked at me like I was crazy and told me to get in the shower. I shrugged it off, showered and got ready for bed. The next day I had an idea since there were extra biscuits leftover from breakfast. I took two of them and put jelly on both. Put them in a paper sandwich baggie and put them on a stump near the area where I heard the noise from. It was just on the other side of the boundary fence between our woods and our neighbor Tim's woods. I had the 45 holstered on me, so I wasn't afraid. I came back by toward evening and saw the bag was gone. Nowhere to be found. Squirrels would have torn the bag open and left it there and taken the food. I just assumed that the hermit guy took it. Every now and then, I would put an apple or some veggies from our garden in a bag there. They would always disappear with no trace of the bags.

33

PERFECT GAME

Age 15

I had been playing baseball every summer since I was five years old. Our Little League team was a decent team over the first eight years. Our thirteen-year-old and over Junior League team that I was on for the last two seasons were headed up to Green Lake for a game. It was about a forty-five-minute drive. I was still fifteen and couldn't drive, so a teammate, Marty, had his license. He asked if Matt and I would ride with him. I said, "Sure." When he came to pick me up, Matt was already in the car. The problem was that it was only a two small seat Mazda. Marty said, "You both will fit." We squeezed in and it was a long drive. We got there and couldn't wait to get out. We all got loosened up. Coach gave me the game ball and said, "Let's go, J Bird." I had my catcher Grady get me ready to pitch. As we were warming up, I kept throwing the ball in the dirt and it was getting past Grady. He was getting a little irritated. Then I heard a voice that sounded familiar. It was my dad. He had been gone playing golf in Green Lake earlier in the day. He had been to only one of my games in Briggsville over the last several years. He sat right behind the backstop so he could see my pitches and was cheering me on.

We were the away team, so we got to hit first. We were able to score a run in the 1st inning. Then as I started to warm up, I was feeling better and had good control of all my pitches. Not a single Green Lake hitter got on base. We were able to score another run in the 2nd inning. I struck out the side in the 2nd. Our offense then hit a dry spell. We couldn't score any runs for a few innings. My coach said, "You got to hold them, kid." Their first hitter hit the ball hard to the shortstop and Matt made a great play and caught the line drive. My dad yelled, "That's too good of a pitch. Keep the ball down in the zone!" In the 7th inning, we got a few more runs to make it 5-0. All we had to do was hold them. The first hitter was the same kid that hit it hard to short earlier. I didn't want to give him anything good, but he watched as three balls were called. My dad was yelling, "You got this!" I had no choice but to go right after him at this point. He watched two strikes go by. Now it was a full count, and he fouled the next pitch back to the backstop. Grady called for a fastball, and I threw it right by him. Whew! That was close! My team was getting really excited. I was laser-focused and struck out the next two hitters as well to end the game. We shook hands with the other team, and they were asking me how did I learn to throw so well? I didn't know what to say other than I was lucky. I didn't realize until after the game when my coach had all the guys on the team sign the ball and give it to me. There was only one out recorded by Matt for his play at short. The rest were all strikeouts. Twenty in total! The ball read:

Briggsville 5 Green Lake 0
7 Innings
20 Strikeouts
0 Walks
0 Baserunners
Jacob Fischer
"Complete Perfect Game!"

I didn't even know there was such a thing!
My dad came up from behind with tears in his eyes; he just gave

me a big hug. He never hugs us. I was a little shocked and he said, "Proud of you, boy!" He patted me on the back and said, "I'll see you at home." He gave me $10 out of his pocket and said, "Go celebrate!"

My coach loaded everyone in the cars, and we headed to a burger joint to celebrate. He bought the whole team burgers, fries, root beer and ice cream! I was on top of the world! My coach even had the game results published in the local newspaper. My mom proudly cut out the article and put it in a scrapbook. Until then, I didn't realize that I could make my parents proud by playing a game.

34

FOREST FIRE

Age 15

It's now late summer and it's we've had very little rain over the last few months. All the farmers are being hit hard with the drought. Crops throughout the area are brown and dying. The soil was so dry it has turned to dust. Only a couple area farmers had irrigation systems for watering their crops. Farmers always know that it's in Mother Nature's hands when it comes down to their crops being successful. Right after eating breakfast, I headed down to the shop to work on some car seats for a Customers' Corvette Stingray when I heard the phone ringing. It was pretty early for any customer to be calling. A few minutes later, my dad called me away from my work and asked me if I had a sharp chain on the chainsaw. I did and had two backups that were also sharp. He told me to get it all together and the gas can and load it all in the truck. I wasn't sure why, but I thought we might be cutting wood for someone. We always helped our neighbors if they needed help. My dad came out of the house and said, "There's a forest fire about half an hour north of us and it's out of control."

I asked, "What do we need to do?"

He said, "You'll be needed to cut trees down to create a fire break."
I was feeling a little unsure of myself, but I couldn't let my dad see it.
We drove toward the fire, and it wasn't long before we could see the
smoke. It was covering the whole sky ahead of us. Once we got near,
we were guided by signal personnel to turn down a road and directed
a mile down to park in the field. We got out of the truck, and they told
my dad to get into a big work truck. My dad said, "I'm not the one you
want." He pointed at me and said, "This boy is as good with a
chainsaw as any logger." The guy looked at me and said, "Ok, kid,
grab your saw and get in." There were three other guys with saws
already in the back of the truck. The driver started the truck and we
headed for the end of the field. They had us get out and grab our
saws. They gave us a quick rundown of safety procedures and how
wide they wanted the fire break to be. He then showed us on a map
where we were responsible for and sent us in different directions.

I was at the head of the row and started cutting down these big
pine trees. After I would cut a few down, a big tractor would haul
them to the center of the field. I got into a good rhythm and was
cutting down about 20 trees an hour. The trees were piling up behind
me. They sent another tractor to help clear all the trees I was cutting
down. A lady would bring us gas, water and snacks ass needed on an
ATV. I was enjoying myself. She said, "You're making the other guys
look, bad kid." I just smiled and got back to it. After about five hours,
the lady came back with turkey sandwiches for us. I was starving. I
ate two sandwiches and a bag of chips. The air was starting to get
smoky. Then a guy came and said the fire was heading our way. I was
getting a little nervous, so I quickly jumped back to work. I was
getting tired now. I had cut almost two hundred trees down. I finally
reach another open field. There was a guy in a truck waiting for me.
He asked if I was good to continue. I nodded and he took me around
the corner to another section of woods. He pointed toward the edge
of the woods and said, "All you got left is to cut a fire break to that
road." I said "Ok" and jumped out, grabbed my stuff and started
cutting again. These were large deciduous trees. Not near as easy as
the pine trees I had been cutting. They were also more dangerous to

cut down. They had big branches going in all directions. I really had to inspect the tree, so I knew where it was going to fall. They were so big we had to cut the tree in half after it was down so the tractors could pull them away. So, this was going to take much longer.

I just kept plugging away at it. As I was finishing, it was starting to get dark. The lady drove me back on the ATV to the fire command center. You could now see a red glow and lots of smoke across the sky. The command center called my dad to come to get me. They thanked me and took down my info. All of us that were helping cut the fire breaks were coming in were so tired we barely spoke. My dad showed up around half an hour later and said, "I heard you were the lead guy out there and cut down the most trees." I said "I don't know." All I knew was I was really sore and doing my best not to fall asleep. We watched the news once we got home and saw that the fire reached where I had been cutting and it was stopped in its tracks. I felt like I had been a part of something special. I knew I would never forget this day for the rest of my life. About a week later, my dad showed me a letter from the DNR and another from the state thanking me for helping out the community in a time of need. My mom put it up on our wall of family pictures for everyone to see.

35

HEARD SOMETHING

Age 15

I t was a beautiful day, and we were waiting for the bus on my first day of High School. I liked Jr. High a lot. I did well in classes, made lots of friends and played 7th. And 8th. Grade football. We had been practicing football ball two a day for the last few weeks. That's once at 7:30 am and then again at 3 pm. Practices were tough, but I was in pretty good shape from all the hard work I did on the farm. I was also timing myself running up the hill toward the woods. Now that school was starting, we were going to only have practice after school each day. I had found my locker and got to my first class. It was history class with my football coach from Jr. High. It was great seeing old friends and hoping for more new friends. After school that day, I had practice and my mom picked me up. We got home and she asked if I could get the mail. I went out to the mailbox on the other side of the road. We rarely had much traffic.

Our German Shepard, Smokey, was racing around me when he started barking up the road toward the east. I looked up and saw a big buck very quickly jump across the road. I could hear him jumping through the woods. I started to look at the mail when Smokey stopped barking and took off, yelping in fear toward the house. I looked at him and thought, what the heck is wrong with him. This dog was afraid of nothing. He even took off after a pack of wild dogs in the past with a cement block tied to his leash. Then I could hear what sounded like an elephant running after this deer. I could hear trees breaking and then nothing. I listened and then I heard what sounded like a big grunt or exhale. I ran into the house and told my dad what I heard. He said maybe it's a bear. I said I didn't see what it was, but it scared Smokey. So, my dad said we weren't going to go check it out since that wasn't our property and we didn't want to intrude on a predator kill. It could be very dangerous. He did call Clark, the owner of the property and told him what happened. Clark went out the next day to check it out and found some trees broken and the carcass of a deer that had been mostly eaten. He came by and said that he didn't find any tracks but said some of the bones were broken. He thought the deer maybe had run into the trees or was tackled into the trees. He thanked us for letting him know and said he'll keep an eye open for any predators. After hearing from Clark, I thought maybe I would go check it out. I, of course, grabbed the rifle and I headed to his woods. It was only about twenty feet into his woods that I could clearly see small tree branches broken. I followed the tree breaks until I found the deer remains. Just like Clark had said, not much left but the hide and bones. It was now smelling like roadkill. I pulled my shirt over my mouth and used a stick to check out the bones. There were several ribs and both rear legs that were broken. Whatever had killed this deer was large and I had to be weary of running into it. The only thing that powerful would have had to be a bear. The only thing is I have never seen a bear anywhere. Not even skat left behind. I guess that's a good thing. Just to make sure that any predators knew that I was coming into the woods, I would always honk the truck horn. I figured this would scare them off while I was up there. Besides that, using the chainsaw and chopping wood made plenty of noise as well. You can never be too careful with Mother Nature.

36

FIRST TIME HUNTING

Age 16

I had just passed my Hunters Safety Gun Class.

I was going deer hunting for the first time in my life. I was very excited to go.

My mom woke me up even earlier than what I'm used to. She made me breakfast and told me to be careful as I left out the door. I had the 30-30 Rifle and the 45-pistol holstered on my hip. I told her to keep the dogs in the house since they would want to follow me. I normally made sure the dogs never left the farm area. We just didn't want the dogs in the woods where they would chase deer. Hunters would shoot any dog on sight if they were either on their property or if they were ever seen chasing deer. Dogs would scare off the deer and put hunting chances at risk. Even when I would be up in the woods, I wouldn't allow the dogs past the farm area.

It was still dark, and I couldn't see now that I was past the yard light. I pulled out my small flashlight. I just needed to see the trail ahead of me. I was about halfway up the hill when I heard my mom let out one of the dogs. Ahead of me, the woods were completely silent. I had never been in the woods this early. I thought of going to the bottom of our upper field and cutting across without going into the woods. The spot I was heading to was just about fifty feet into the woods. An area where I've always seen lots of deer. As I was crossing the field, I heard something about fifty yards behind me. It was running fast. Then I heard yelping. It was heading straight for me. I pulled up my gun, took the safety off and pointed it in the direction it was coming from. It was still pitch black out. Then out of nowhere, I get my legs cut out from under me. I was on the ground. It was our other dog, Brewski. He took off yelping. I instantly yelled, "Get back to the house!" Then I heard from that same direction something big stopping and then these heavy footsteps getting farther away. I still couldn't see anything. I could hear it run through the trees and off toward the neighbor's woods to the east. The only thing I could think that it might be was a big buck. At this point, I was pissed off at the dog for scaring off what might have been the big buck I was hoping for. I just shook it off and headed for my spot. I sat there for hours, listening and hoping for the "big buck" to walk by. I saw squirrels, chipmunks and even a bobcat walking by. It started to rain, but I was determined not to go back without a deer. Then I could hear something coming over the ridge. I took off my safety and readied for a shot.

There were four does slowly walking and eating. I was hoping that there would be at least one buck following them. Sure enough, there was one, but he was too far away. I couldn't get a clean shot. They all jumped over the fence and headed into Brett's woods behind ours. After not seeing anything for about another hour, I decided to walk back up through the length of our woods. There was nothing going on, so I headed back for the house. It was still raining, so I was soaked. As I walked out of the woods, I could see where I had walked this morning knocking down the tall grass all the way through the upper field. I walked over to the point where Brewski had run into me. I followed his tracks back toward the east to see if I could see if there were any deer tracks. I didn't see any deer tracks, but I found what looked like two piles of dirt that looked as if someone planted both feet to stop and slide sideways. It was raining still, so it was hard to tell. I then thought, was this a person or a hunter that was chasing the dog? I just knew I was cold and hungry. I changed into warm clothes and grabbed something to eat. My mom asked, "How did it go?"

I said, "Brewski probably screwed my hunt up."

She said, "Well, he has been hiding in the bedroom since he came back in." I told her what had happened. She said, "Maybe Brewski was chasing a deer and a hunter was chasing him?"

I said, "Ya, but he was on our property. It was all just weird." I went to check on Brewski. Sure enough, he looked up at me with eyes of fear. I just said, "That's what you get for chasing deer! Don't do that again!" I called him out to the living room. He was very reluctant to come out. I then got him to go outside. He went to the bathroom and ran back into the house right away. I guess this hunter really shook him up. I figured he'd never do anything like that again!

37

VOICES

Age 16

It was a cold crisp Saturday morning in November. There was no snow yet, so I was still able to get up the big hill to go cut wood. I headed toward the far back of the woods with the truck and trailer. After cutting wood all morning, I heard my dad whistle for lunch, so I started to walk down to the farm to eat. The weird thing was I heard a whistle just like his coming from deeper in the back of the woods in response. So, I whistled the same. Then I heard the whistle from the back of the woods again. It was coming from Brett's woods that bordered the back of our woods. It wasn't an echo. It was mimicking my whistle. I whistled again but then no response. I tried again a couple times but nothing. If it was an echo, I would have heard it after all of my whistles as well. Maybe the Stranger was back?

Perplexed, I left everything there and ran down to the farm to eat. By the time I got down to the farm, my dad had already laid down for his hour or so midday nap. I ate and hung out with my mom watching her soap Opera while my dad took his nap. When he got up, I walked back up into the woods to continue working. As I was walking up to the truck, I could see a big ten-point buck along the fence line. It wasn't looking at me. Then I hear off to the right a mumbled voice. I couldn't understand what they were saying. The deer was fixated on the direction I heard the voice from. Then I heard off to the left in a slightly higher pitch more mumbled talking going on. I thought it could be Brett and his son Gus. I listened a little more and the voice on the right said something again and then the left responded again. The deer responded toward each voice. I could hear them loud and clear. I thought maybe Brett or Gus were bow hunting or had possibly let some hunters onto their land. I heard a branch break, and the deer took off. I then thought I should let them know I was there. Just in case they were bow hunting. I know I didn't want to get shot! I just yelled out..." Gus? Brett? It's Jacob! Is everything ok?" I thought if this was them, then they would surely respond. Yet I heard nothing. I repeated myself even louder. "Hello! Brett? Gus?" Still nothing. I was puzzled. The voices almost sounded like a foreign language. Even though I could hear them loud and clear, I couldn't make out any words at all. I kept my eye open the rest of the afternoon, but I didn't see or hear anything. The woods were very quiet the rest of the day. I finished loading the truck and trailer and headed back down to the farm and stacked it by the old barn wall.

The next day I went down to Brett's farm while he was milking his cows and asked him if they were up in their woods behind our land. He said, "No, why?" I said, "I could hear these mumbled voices and I called out and no one responded." He then said, "Did you see anything?" He had this weird smile on his face when he asked that question. I said, "No. Maybe some hunters on your property?" He said, "Maybe." He then said You better be careful in those woods." I said, "I am, I always have a gun on me at all times up there." He said, "Good!" I then told him that my dad and I had found a rock ledge last year that looked like someone was hanging out up there. He then said, "Well, maybe my brother (Levi, the old owner) wasn't completely crazy!" I didn't know what he meant about that, but I headed back home with more questions than answers.

38

DRIVERS LICENSE

Age 16

Now that I was 16 and I could drive (legally), my dad was sending me on errands all the time. I always wanted to drive, but now it was work. I would previously drive to town sometimes to get something for mom at the General Store, or my dad would send me to the tavern to grab a twelve-pack of beer or cigarettes. Yep! They just knew it was for my dad. Things were a little different back then. But now I had to drive to customers' homes or businesses to pick up furniture or car seats and even sometimes a car. On one of my first trips, I went to Lake Delton to pick up a squad car to replace the carpet. It was a little weird driving a cop car. There wasn't any snow on the roads yet, so my dad felt safe sending me to run most of his errands. I think it was cheaper for him to drink at home versus paying bar prices. Plus, he had put several of our vehicles into the ditch over the years, driving intoxicated.

My younger brother Lonnie was now putting all the home furniture back together and I did all the auto upholstery. We only had a couple cows, three pigs and five chickens left on the farm. My dad was dwindling down the farm and was focused on the shop. It had turned into a very nice business. Hard work, but he always had cheap labor. Us boys, my mom and himself. We had used auto dealers, bars, restaurants, boat companies, all using us to reupholster anything that had material on it. We even had a deal with a large restaurant chain, Country Kitchen, in the entire state. So, my dad had me running constantly. My little brother Dean now was helping take apart a lot of the furniture. He was the baby of the family and sort of acted like that. He was plain lazy and always resisted work.

Whenever we had spare time, Lonnie and I would play basketball or one on one tackle football games in the front yard of the old farmhouse. Not a lot of time to play and be "normal kids," but we made the most of it. On this day, as Lonnie and I were practicing punting the football back and forth by the old farmhouse, he had punted it and it landed by the apple tree on the side of the corn field. Since we only needed a small amount of corn for the few animals, my dad had leased out the field to our neighbor Brett to grow corn. Brett would give us enough of the harvest to get through the year. Brett was about to pick the field the next week. As I approached the football, I could hear this grunting coming from the cornfield and the dry stalks being thrashed through. I thought that it was a deer, but then I could see the top of someone's head and thought this must be that tall guy again. The stalks were about 7 feet tall, and I could see his whole head above them. He was pretty far away, and it was getting dark out, but I yelled out, "Get off our property!" Immediately he stopped, and it looked like he was turning around, but I couldn't see or hear him after that. I yelled out again, "And stay off our property!" I then added, "We're calling the sheriff too!" Lonnie then came around the house and asked, "Who are you yelling at?" I said, "It's that tall guy again!" Lonnie replied, "We should tell mom and dad!" We both ran in and told our mom since our dad was already passed out in bed.

She then said, "Maybe we should call the sheriff." I told her, "I think he lives in the back of Tim's woods off to the east of ours." Mom then called and talked to the Sheriff, and he told her he would check it out. We never heard a word about it after that.

39

WHOOPS AND ROCKS

Age 16

Spring has arrived again, and I had time to get back up into the woods to start preparing a woodpile for next year. We again had a pretty severe Wisconsin winter and we almost had run out of wood again. We went through quite a bit with needing wood for the shop and the garage where I worked the last several months. The business had really taken me away last year from stockpiling what we needed. We actually had to cut down a couple trees near the farm to get through till Spring. My dad sent me on a mission to make sure that we had plenty of wood chopped for next winter. He also decided that this would be the last year that we would have any of the animals. I was sad about that, but they were just not worth the work any longer. I had a favorite pig, "Frank," that I would let into the house once in a while. He would come in and sit in front of the TV and snort as though he understood what was going on. Frank was like one of the dogs. He liked to follow me around the farm and had quite the personality. My dad would hear us upstairs and yell from the shop, "You better not be up there watching TV! And that damn pig better not be in the house!" Frank would look at me and I would turn off the

TV. Frank would get all upset, squeal and run out of the house, slamming the screen door. Then my dad would yell, "Quit slamming the damn door!" It was all pretty comical and made me chuckle.

I then grabbed the chainsaw and filled it up with gas, oil and sharpened the chain. I would then load up the trailer with backup gas and oil and head for the woods. I also had my dad's 45 holstered and the 30/30 by me on the seat. I parked toward the back of the woods and noticed what looked like a Tepee. It was a structure of about five or six smaller trees, all laying against each other. I had never seen that before and as I looked, I couldn't figure out how they had just naturally fallen like that. It seemed as though they had been placed by someone. One of the trees had the roots sticking up at the top. Not sure why or who would have done that. The only thing I could think of was the Stranger did it. I really didn't care at the time and thought to myself that it was "easy wood". I just grabbed the chainsaw and said,""oh well! I've got work to do." I started cutting them down and throwing them into the trailer. Then I heard what sounded like a whoop. I wasn't sure what it was. It sounded like what I thought was an owl in the past. It reminded me more like a chimp noise that I had heard on one of my favorite shows, Wild Kingdom. I kept working and moved over to a big fallen tree. I cut it into logs and started splitting it into smaller pieces with an ax. Then I heard the whoop again! I scanned the area where it had come from but couldn't see anything. So, I whooped back. Then I heard it a third time. I still couldn't see anything. I figured it must be some sort of bird. I kept splitting the wood and loading it into the trailer. Then I heard something hit the truck. It really didn't alarm me. I thought maybe it was a stick that had fallen from a tree. Then I heard something go zipping by me. It hit some leaves as it came in toward me, so I knew what direction it came from. It was coming from Brett's woods across the fence line. At this point, I knew it wasn't a bird or squirrel throwing rocks at me. I found the rock and with all my might, I launched it back. I heard it hit a tree solid about one hundred feet away. I then yelled, "You hit me with a rock you're going to piss me off." I didn't hear anything. I followed it with, "I have a gun and I suggest you knock it off!" Still nothing. I finished filling the trailer and took it down to the farm. I unloaded and stacked the load. I went in and said to my dad, "There is someone throwing rocks at me from Brett's woods." I told him I threw it back, but I didn't see or hear anything else. I didn't mention the whoops I heard since I thought this was some sort of bird. He seemed slightly concerned, but he said, "Just stay down here and get some work done in the shop." As I was walking away, he said, "Next time, just fire a warning shot in the air." Whoever it is will get the message." I just thought to myself, whoever it is is just messing around. I didn't ever feel like my life was in danger. I didn't want to possibly kill someone either!

40

TERROR

Age 16

I had just played our last baseball game of the summer and was riding my bike home. I rode part of the way together with Mason, who turned off on their road about halfway. He was telling me that he would sometimes ride the snowmobile trails near his house with Ken, another friend of ours. I thought that was a great idea since we had a trail that ran along the east end of our property. It was just on the other side of the fence on Tim's side. During the winter, we would have people drive their snowmobiles by on the trail. Not very many, though. I thought I would see if it was clear enough to ride my bike on. The trails tend to get overgrown with brush, fallen branches and sometimes, a whole tree will fall across it throughout the summer. I got home and dropped off my baseball equipment and grabbed a glass of water. My dad asked, "Where are you going?" It was Sunday, so I had the afternoon off. I told him, "I'm going to ride my bike a little." He was having a few drinks, so I could tell he was getting tipsy already. He then told me as he pointed toward the edge of the woods, "Before dark, go get the cow that's tied to the tree on the top of the hill and put it back in the pen." We only had one cow left and we would tie it up around the farm where there was fresh grass for grazing.

I first took my bike down to the garage and made sure the tires had good air pressure. It's a lot easier to ride on dirt paths if the tires are nice and full. I also wanted to check the chain since the weekend before I was at the lake and broke it when I tried to ride up a big hill. I pushed too hard, and the chain broke, causing my foot to fly off the pedal and hit the ground. It wasn't a pleasant experience. I didn't want to do that again. Plus, I had to walk my bike four miles home. Not fun! The chain was tight and the tires full. As I headed up the road, I could see the cow tied up on the hillside near the woods. I had to decide, do I ride the trail that went behind our property or do I turn right and ride the trail downhill. The trail to the right was along with open fields and mostly flat. Not the most exciting scenery. I chose to go left and ride behind our property. It was going to be hilly and more fun to zoom up and down those rolling hills. Right away, I would have to ride up a steep hill to get to a high point before the rolling hills would start. That was going to be the hard part. So I got up good speed on the road and started making my way up. I kept my head down and flew right up to the top. After the first hill, there was going to be a small dip and then a small incline. As I crested the hill, I saw something move about twenty-five feet in front of me. It was hairy. I saw a big hairy leg and as I lifted my head, I was looking at the biggest living creature that I've ever seen. I immediately hit the brakes and started sliding sideways. It seemed at that moment everything was moving in slow motion. Instant fear came over me. I couldn't take my eyes off it. I was terrified of what I was looking at. As I skidded closer, I looked straight into the huge orangish eyes of this creature. It had this look of what I would describe as surprise.

It was partially behind a large tree. It was at least eight feet tall and looked almost human but so much bigger and very muscular. It was like I was looking at a very hairy naked human being. As soon as I stopped, I was peddling as hard as I could to get away. I was saying to myself, "If the chain breaks...I'm dead!" I didn't look back, but I was just hoping this thing didn't come after me. I peddled as fast as I could back down the hill. Still not looking back, I hit the road, skidding sideways, almost wiping out. I headed straight for the house riding the bike right to the back door. I ran inside, closing the door in complete panic. My dad was sitting there at the kitchen table. He yelled, "What the hell's going on?"

I was out of breath and said, "There's a Bigfoot right over the top of the hill."

"A what?"

"A huge hairy Bigfoot. I almost ran into him on the trail!"

My dad said, "Horse shit!

"I'm serious, Dad!"

He said, "Go get that cow off the hill and put it back in the pen." My response? I said, "No way," and ran downstairs to the shop that had a window that could see that side of the hill. I could see the cow! It was nervously pacing back and forth and pulling on the rope, trying to get free. I could hear my dad yelling for me, but there was no way I was going up there. Then after a few minutes, I could see my dad walking up the hill toward the cow. He had a pistol in his hand and peered around the area a little before walking the cow back down. I could hear him talking to my mom upstairs. He was telling her what I said. He told my mom that the cow was spooked when he went to get it. I couldn't believe he didn't believe me! He told my mom it might have been a black bear. I would have been scared of a black bear, but this was no bear. This creature had a human face. I was still trembling. I couldn't stop staring out the window. My dad finally drank himself to sleep, so I made my way upstairs. I said, "Mom, I know what I saw! It was huge! It wasn't a bear! It was a Bigfoot!" She said, "Are you sure it wasn't a bear?" I said, "Not a chance, Mom! It looked like The Incredible Hulk (a popular TV show) but hairy everywhere." She didn't seem to believe me either. She just said, "Well, whatever it was, just be careful of it." It was getting late, so I headed to bed, very frustrated that no one was taking me seriously. I couldn't stop thinking it could reach right through the window and grab me. I was truly scared and reliving the incident over and over in my head, trying to make sense of it. I lay awake until it started to get light out. Finally, I passed out. About an hour later, my dad was waking us up. I was so tired. Mentally and physically.

41

FEAR

Age 16

The next morning when my dad yelled for us to get up, I had felt a lot on edge. I barely slept and for the first time ever, I didn't want to leave the house. I walked out to eat breakfast, thinking my dad was going to grill me about what happened yesterday. He didn't say a word. I was relieved when he wanted me to run to Baraboo to pick up some car seats. I was happy to get away. Once I got back with the seats, I offered to take them apart right away. He said, "Ok." I continued busy around the farm. I couldn't shake the feeling that I was being watched from the woods. I also couldn't get this thing's face out of my mind. Especially its eyes. Its eyes were not of a threat but more like I startled him by quietly riding up on him. It had every chance to grab me, but it didn't. It remained motionless. I think it was checking out the cow we had tied up just over the edge of the hill. I don't think it heard me coming and I surprised it. The more I thought about and processed this, the more I realized that this creature was there watching me all along. It literally had hundreds of opportunities to hurt me if it wanted to. Now I know why the horses never wanted to go near the woods. There were so many clues, but I always assumed these incidents were always having humans involved. Starting from shortly after moving here when I thought I saw a really tall person at the edge of the woods when I was a little kid to all the footprints we've seen from time to time, to the rock-throwing, the tree pushed over the trail, the loud grunts, the whoops, the whistles, the screaming lady, the trees stacked like a tepee, my cabin torn apart, the rock clapping, the missing pig, the tree knocks when I thought was someone cutting wood, the torso I thought I saw, the tall person walking through the corn and so on. I now believe that the weird mumbling-sounding voices I heard were at least two of these creatures. Definitely a male that I ran into face to face and possibly a female. Who knows, maybe even more.

I did finally go back into the woods the next spring. I was even more alert about my surroundings whenever I did. I cut wood all summer and kept my guns by my side. I never saw, heard or smelled anything that I had experienced in the past. In a way, I wanted to see this creature again to confirm in my mind that I wasn't crazy! However, I think that once I saw it that they immediately moved on to a safer location. Somewhere deeper into the woods, away from people. It felt almost the same around the woods as when one of my grade school friends moved to another state. I missed the presence of this creature as I missed my friend. I even put some biscuits on the stump a couple times to only sit there for a couple days until I found the bag chewed apart and laying on the ground with the biscuits gone.

All I know is I moved away from the farm shortly after I turned eighteen due to my dad's drinking and abusive nature. I immediately got a job and an apartment in the Dells. It felt good to be on my own and to actually make some money compared to the twenty dollars a week I was making working full time on the farm. It was a factory job, but I was making that much every four hours of work. I worked there until I finished my last semester of high school. I was proud of myself to be the first of us boys to graduate and I did it living on my own and supporting myself.

That summer, I decided to work at Paul Bunyan restaurant and

Noah's Ark water park, where I really enjoyed working with so many other employees and customers. Talk about a turnaround work atmosphere versus the life I knew on the farm growing up. At the end of the summer, I moved with a friend to Madison and started putting myself through college.

As I think back, I feel sad at times about my experiences on the farm. I felt as though my dad had wasted so much of our time drinking and being angry. All I wanted was a loving and caring family. I'm sure he loved us. He just didn't show it. His style was tough love and the school of hard knocks. He did end up stopping his drinking and smoking after a trip to the hospital. The doctor told him that he had to stop or he won't live another year. I am proud of him for his strength to be able to overcome his illness and bless us for another six years of what I would describe as a semi-normal relationship. Something that I always desired my whole life growing up. Even though our meetings after that were only during holiday visits that only lasted a few hours.

I also have always wondered if I may have had a friend or friends from afar in the woods. What if I didn't take that ride on the trail that day, they would not have had to move on. I wonder, even today, where is he or them now? At times I even wonder how close I was to danger or was I ever in danger? I will never know. Due to people maybe thinking that I'm completely crazy, I've only told a couple very close people these life experiences. Heck, my own parents didn't believe me at the time. I didn't even believe in this creature until I saw it with my own eyes. You want to tell everyone, but you know deep inside that you can't. All I knew was that seeing is knowing. Seeing something like this changes your thought process of life. I'm really not sure how this creature has been able to stay off the known species category even today. I just knew that they were under my nose and after fifteen years, I accidentally ran into one. There is this weight that looms over you after experiencing something like this. I'm hoping that writing this sets me free.

Over the last almost forty years since I left the farm, there are fifteen more families that have populated the area living on our country block. Also, many of the nearby farmers that are still operating have had loggers come in and clear cut much of the forests surrounding the farms for more fields to grow crops. There is less and less area for these creatures to live as humans gradually keep occupying their habitats. I'm sure it was just a matter of time before they would have had to move on anyway. I didn't realize that several of the things I had happen throughout my life on the farm were related until I had seen documentaries on TV of experiences that others have had. Every time I finally realized the reality of each incident, the hairs would stand up on my arms. I truly believe that I was, most of the time, just a curiosity of the creatures. For the rest of the world who believes, I will tell them that there is a big difference between believing and knowing.

www.ingramcontent.com/pod-product-compliance
Lightning Source LLC
Chambersburg PA
CBHW070125030426
42335CB00016B/2273